THE OFF-GRID SOLAR POWER BIBLE

[4 in 1] A Step-by-Step Guide to Design, Install, and Maintain Solar Energy Systems for RVs, Cabins, Boats, and Tiny Homes

Peter Cress

Table of Contents

Introduction

When you choose to live off the grid, you are no longer reliant on your power company's electrical supply. Benefits include no longer having to pay large sums to your power company and no longer experiencing power outages.

You've probably heard of solar panels being used to power your home, but have you ever considered using them to power your tiny house? Consider living off the grid and generating electricity on a budget. You've got this! It is possible, and it is not as difficult as many people believe. The key is to find a few parts that complement each other.

A completely self-sufficient solar PV (Photovoltaic) power system that provides electrical grid independence from the utility grid is known as an off-grid solar power system or stand-alone solar power system. It typically consists of photovoltaic panels, batteries, an inverter, and various other components to deliver power where it is needed.

Solar power's discovery is our ticket to regaining control over what we allow into our lives. It is produced from a natural resource that is abundant and free and consistently produces as much electricity as is needed for our homes.

Solar power systems are one-time investments that provide a hundredfold return for the rest of our lives.

Solar power systems help supply electricity to remote homes while saving significant household money. Installing an electric pole close to the house or extending wires from the closest main utility grid access point are much more expensive than using solar energy. In other words, solar energy enables independent homes to achieve complete self-sufficiency by generating their own heat for showers, cooking, and any other necessary practical electrical requirements.

In this book, I hope to provide you with the most up-to-date information and practical advice for building your solar power system for remote homes. Making your own off-grid solar power system may appear to be a daunting task requiring a science degree; however, this is not the case. All you'll need is some basic math skills and an open mind.

Many may be wary of going utterly off-grid due to the high costs of owning one of these systems. Despite being substantially more expensive than on-grid solar power systems (which still rely on the power grid), off-grid solar power systems are still a good investment. Reduce your power demands by switching to energy-saving electrical appliances, machines, and accessories. This is a brilliant way to make your system much cheaper.

This book presents the basic materials and methods required for forming a stage of informing in the design and construction of solar power plants, referred to as Solar Electric Supply. Only photoelectric conversion is considered for solar energy supply (photovoltaic, photoelectric). The book intends to improve the skills of design and construction specialists working in industrial and civil engineering to build a photovoltaic system for your home.

Furthermore, solar energy is the source of all other available energies on the planet, including wind, fossil fuel, wave, hydroelectric, biomass, geothermal, and tidal energy. Because of the energy the sun releases daily, it is a renewable, available, inexhaustible, and clean source. Solar energy is captured and converted into electricity (via photovoltaic solar panels) or thermal energy (through solar thermal energy). The sun's energy can be converted in three ways: solar photovoltaic, thermal, and thermodynamic. Let’s get started.

BOOK 1

Chapter 1: Basics of Off-Grid Living

Most people live off the grid to save energy and live in a natural environment. Off-grid living, without a doubt, necessitates some initial planning and investment. If you want to start living without relying on electricity, here is a guide to help you:

- **Choose the right location to live:** If you intend to harness the natural resources of wind, water, and solar power to generate electricity, you will need to live in an area where these resources are plentiful and easily accessible. Off-grid living necessitates the construction of an off-grid home in a sunny and windy location.

- **Save up for the initial investment:** Such a lifestyle frequently necessitates investing in a home that uses independent energy resources or building an energy-efficient house for yourself. All of this necessitates significant investment and planning.
- **Stay in an off-grid society:** If you want to stay off-grid but cannot find land with abundant wind, solar, and water power to harness, you can always choose one of the pre-built communities that follow a self-sufficient lifestyle.
- **Install a septic tank:** To live entirely off the grid, purchase land that allows you to draw water from a well. Install a septic tank to complete this task. All of these are required for effective wastewater management.
- **Invest in an energy-efficient plan:** Doing some preliminary planning is a profitable and efficient way to begin living off the grid. Invest in customized plans that include the annual production of up to 10,000 kWh of electricity. You can also use solar panels, hydro energy, and other forms of energy storage.
- **Purchase storage devices such as generators:** Backup systems, such as propane generators, will be required to store the renewable energy you harvest. Save money for such systems and clear out storage space for them.
- **Drill a household well:** To live off the grid, you must rely on natural water resources such as rain and groundwater. If you grow crops on your land, you may need to drill a household well or purchase cisterns for rainwater collection.
- **Choose solar kits:** Installing solar thermal panels for your home or commercial space is the most effective way to reduce energy consumption and live entirely off the grid. They significantly reduce your energy bills, whether used alone or in conjunction with an electric supply.
- **Begin composting:** Living off the grid entails providing a garbage collection service for your home. You can compost or recycle most of your household waste and take the rest to your local dump by composting or recycling.
- **Limit overall electric consumption:** If your livelihood is dependent on electronics, there are a few things you can do to reduce overall consumption. Install energy

backups, such as generators, and reduce the use of unnecessary electric appliances at home, such as dryers, microwaves, and video game consoles.

Living off the grid is a wise lifestyle choice that will likely bear fruit in future generations as the world faces enormous energy issues. Living off the grid is not only environmentally friendly and futuristic but also saves money in the long run.

Benefits of Off-Grid Living

People who have chosen an off-the-grid lifestyle a few years ago would tell you that this new lifestyle of theirs has outweighed all those new comforts that city life had offered. Also, you will enjoy long-term benefits such as the low amount of power outages, lesser energy expenses, better environmental knowledge, and lesser dependence on naturally occurring fuels. If you plan to choose this natural style of lifestyle, then you must know its array of benefits in detail.

There are No Power Outages

The power of your off-the-grid home will remain intact even if there is a storm with lightning or heavy snowfall. You will be able to get hot water and lighting in your home because you will have BP solar panels and wind turbines to provide you with natural power. It also means that your loved ones will be kept warm during the colder months, and your work or productivity will not be disrupted.

Improved Environmental Awareness

When you have alternative energy systems, you can update your knowledge in the best way possible by learning various methods to help you achieve hands-on education about the environment. You will learn about the patterns of solar energy as well as the changes in the weather. You will understand how to use solar energy to keep warm during the winter and wind energy to keep cool at night. You can do your laundry on a hot day and hang it to dry using the sun's natural energy. You will also learn more ways to conserve natural energy for later use.

Reduces Our Reliance on Fossil Fuels

When you choose an off-grid lifestyle, you are not reliant on power companies for energy. It also implies that you should be concerned about rising power rates. You will also reduce your carbon footprint by only using green and renewable energy in your home. When compared to the emissions of fossil fuels when burned, the fossil fuels emit more pollution and have higher levels of carbon emissions. Even though it will take a bit of time for you to adjust to the new off-grid style, you can be sure of being more responsible towards the environment. It would make your lifestyle highly rewarding, making it worth your sacrifices in the grid-tied living.

What is an Off-Grid Solar Power System?

An off-grid solar power system is a collection of solar panels that produces electricity for small households or industrial sites without being connected to the community grid. It is self-sufficient and self-sufficient. This system is powered by energy stored in a battery bank. Electric currents from this off-grid solar system charge and maintain this power bank. Lost electrical energy in the battery is thus restored for future use.

Off-grid solar structures must be outfitted with the appropriate solar panels to maintain an optimal electric current capable of powering your appliances. The panels should be installed in sufficient sunlight to avoid shades that could interfere with their functionality. The rest of the system may suffer if your photovoltaic panels are covered.

You'll need this solar power structure to reduce your energy bills. It is preferable to camping or vacationing in your RVs, cars, boats, vans, or living in a small apartment. The system can power your appliances and lighting and charge your computer devices. However, before beginning the project, you should assess your need for an off-grid solar array.

When understanding any type of power generation technology, we must remember that power is influenced not only by its generation but also by its distribution. Currently, the power eco-system is characterized by centralized generation (regardless of generation method) fed into a national grid and transported over long distances. This has a two-fold impact. The first is that expanding or maintaining this grid requires a significant capital investment. The second point is that there are significant inefficiencies at work here: you have to generate significantly more electricity to meet the needs of a community when you have to transport that energy over wires because a significant amount is wasted in transmission. Consider this: if water pipes were naturally porous (this is hypothetical to make a point), you would lose more water as the pipe distance increased (traveling from the source to use). As a result, if the water source were two doors away, you would lose less water than if the source was two towns away. Part of the water seeps out of the pipe with each length of pipe traveled. As a result, the water plant must process more water to compensate for the loss of this water. Water processing is costly.

The functions of this system will generally be the same regardless of the design and products you end up with. Your solar power system will work by absorbing natural sunlight and converting photons into usable energy. Because of the scientific process, these systems are frequently referred to as photovoltaic or P.V., solar power systems.

Installing these systems can reduce your reliance on the community power grid, which provides electricity to cool, heat, light, and operate your home. As a result, you will have a clean, renewable energy source that requires little maintenance after the initial installation. Once your solar system is paid off, you will have free energy for years, if not decades.

Solar power systems use a grid-tied method in urban areas, like residential neighborhoods. This means they are still connected to the primary power grid that can be initiated for backup energy. This way, once your solar reserves run out at night, you will still have energy from another source. Yes, you will receive an energy bill, but it will still be significantly lower than using the power grid 24/7. So, you will not have to worry about losing power in the middle of the night while watching a long movie or doing some extra work in your living room.

On the other hand, in more rural areas with underdeveloped land, the homes will have to rely on an off-grid system because there will be no primary power grid. As a result, they will have to rely on solar alone once they choose this route. I will not get into the main components of a solar power system.

Now think about this same thing in electricity terms. The power generation company has to generate more electricity than is being used because it has to transmit that electricity over inefficient cables over long distances.

The idea behind this is to have a farm of solar panels and then connect that power generation ability to the existing grid so that the power can be transmitted to the end-user.

The second method is to distribute the solar generation ability and allow each end user to generate what he needs when he needs it and then push what he doesn't use back to the grid so that others can use it. This is the personal solar generation capability.

In this book, we will be focusing on this personal generation capability and how to go about literally getting off the grid by doing that.

How Does an Off-Grid Solar Power System Work?

The idea of running your remote home with electricity not regulated by utility companies is appealing. Many homeowners are looking for the independence and sustainability that off-grid solar power systems can provide. This technology is now readily available and affordable for many households to utilize. The journey of how solar energy is translated into electricity is not complicated to understand. You can finally understand the importance of those glistening glass panels you frequently see on rooftops by reading the complete explanation of how off-grid solar systems operate that followsConversion of Electric Current

.

The Solar Panels will be Activated by Sunlight

Solar panels comprise a layer of silicon photovoltaic cells, a metal frame, and a clear glass casing surrounded by a special film and wiring. Many homeowners prefer to group multiple panels in a series on rooftops to collect as much energy as possible. The photovoltaic cells are in charge of absorbing as much sunlight as possible during the day.

The Photovoltaic Cells Make an Electric Current

A thin semiconductor wafer of two silicon layers is embedded within each PV cell. This wafer's one layer is positively charged while the other is negatively charged, resulting in an electric field. When sunlight strikes a PV cell, energy is generated within the cell, allowing electrons to separate from atoms within the semiconductor wafer. These freed electrons are powered by the electric field that surrounds the wafer, and this power is what generates an electric current.

Conversion of Electric Current

Though sunlight has been effectively converted by the solar panels into an electric current, this current still needs to be transformed into one that can power your home. Direct current (or DC) power is what solar panels produce; but, in order to turn on the lights at home, you must convert it to alternating current (or AC) voltage. This process is enabled by using a technological device known as an inverter. One inverter can be used for the entire system in modern solar power systems, or a few single microinverters can be placed behind the solar panels.

Alternating Current Electricity Powers Your Home

Once the inverter transforms a DC electric current into an AC electric current, the current will pass via the house's electrical panel (the main electricity switchboard). As a result, it is distributed throughout the home, providing power to all electrical appliances. This type of electricity is identical to the electricity you receive from the utility company. Furthermore, no changes to the home setup are required.

Differences Between Off-Grid, On-Grid, And Hybrid Solar Systems

Solar power systems are in three categories depending on their structures, features, and functionalities. They are off-grid solar power systems, on-grid solar power systems, and hybrid solar systems. Most homeowners prefer to live off the grid; others choose to connect their solar arrays on the grid, while others maintain the hybrid solar system.

Now, look at these different types and their benefits to homeowners.

Off-Grid Solar Power System

Off-grid solar systems are not connected to the power grid. They are classified as independent or standalone solar systems. Starting this type of electricity project necessitates the purchase of several accessories, including a power generating set for backup and a storage battery.

To keep your photovoltaic system operational, you should replace a battery power bank every ten years. However, you should be aware that batteries can reduce the efficiency of a solar power system and are also costly.

On-Grid Solar Power System

On-grid solar systems are power networks linked to the utility power grid. It is also known as a grid-tied system or grid back feeding.

Net metering is used in the system, which helps to save money. In some countries, citizens are compensated for sending excess power generated by their solar systems back to the general grid. This is also referred to as net metering. Excess current is no longer stored in batteries for personal use but instead flows to the grid system.

The power grid functions as a virtual battery for storing excess current. However, this case does not need maintenance or battery replacement. Instead, you will benefit from an efficient electricity supply.

On-grid solar power systems need two major pieces of equipment to function correctly. These include power meters and microinverters.

Power Meter

The power meter is also called a net meter or a two-way meter. The device can measure the electric current flowing in two directions. That is, from your house to the grid and then back again. A local utility company should be able to educate you on the functions and features of net metering. A power meter could be given to customers for free or for a small fee. Ensure that your power meter is compatible with net metering.

Microinverters

Each solar panel is fitted with microinverters. However, in the case of central inverters, one inverter could be used for an array of panels. Experience has proven that microinverters are efficient and more functional than central inverters. It is also more expensive. Microinverters are a solution to issues of shading on solar power arrays.

Grid-Tied or Synchronous Inverters

Solar inverters manage and control the voltage and current from photovoltaic panels. They convert direct current from the panels into alternating current. This type of current is suitable for electronics and other electrical equipment.

Grid-tied or synchronous inverters help synchronize the current's frequency and phase to suit and complement the general grid. The nominal frequency is 60 hertz. In this case, the output voltage is adjusted higher than the grid voltage. This adjustment will cause excessive current to flow out to the utility grid.

Hybrid System

This is a hybrid of off-grid and grid-connected solar power systems. In layman's terms, it is an off-grid solar system with backup power. The hybrid solar system can also be a grid-connected solar system with an extra battery bank for storing excess current. If you own an electric vehicle, it is essentially a backup battery on wheels. This is an illustration of a hybrid solar system.

The hybrid solar system is an innovative solar platform that incorporates numerous innovations and new inverters. The system has a high electrical power output at noon. You can use your solar system to power your home, electric vehicle, and other large appliances. Excess electricity can thus be stored in batteries. When electricity tariffs are high, the current could be returned to the grid for higher returns. The hybrid solar system lays the groundwork for a smart grid electricity network.

Hybrid solar stations are cheaper than off-grid solar systems. With this setup, backup generators are not needed. You can even downsize your battery bank. It is cheaper to consume and maintain off-peak electricity from the grid than to buy diesel.

The hybrid solar system is designed to function with special equipment such as a power meter, battery bank, battery-based grid-connected inverter system, DC disconnect, and charge controller.

An Inverter in a Solar System

Grid-tied solar systems cannot function without an inverter. It is a necessity in a solar system setup. Connecting inverters to solar installation transforms direct current electricity into alternating current. It can produce an electrical potential of 240 V. This voltage can power all your household appliances.

Inverters are designed to function constantly as long as the solar power system is functional. In most setups, it is usually the only equipment that develops faults. Most inverter devices come with ten-year warranty service. High-quality inverters that are serviceable can be found on the market. Examples include Sungrow, Fronius, SolarEdge, and ABB.

Benefits of Using Off-Grid Solar Power

Solar power is significantly beneficial when you look at it from a scaled perspective – meaning it has overreaching benefits for all of mankind and the rest of nature because the conventional sources of electricity generation harm the health of living organisms and the environment as a whole. Solar energy can generate electricity in a way that does not have any of these effects, making clean energy a significant reason for the shift to it.

But more importantly, there is one economic reason that most individuals and societies fail to realize. Nonrenewable resources are coming to a point where supply certainty is questioned. Mining and exploration costs are increasing to the point that other forms of energy extraction are becoming comparatively less economical and thus more expensive. That increased cost affects everyone. It translates to higher input costs for manufacturing and thereby higher costs of goods ranging from food to clothing and transportation to housing. Indeed, it touches all layers of the economy.

Aside from rising costs, there is the annoying instability of costs that affect households. The cost of power can fluctuate as time goes by, and as average temperatures rise, the cost of cooling homes and offices is starting to place a demand on the power grid. There are cases where you observe rolling brownouts in neighborhoods with sweltering heat in the summer. A house fitted with supplemental solar power will not be a victim of brownouts or out-and-out power disruption.

Often, we limit ourselves to what we want to use in the home, which may strain the costs of power. With a solar system in the house, we no longer have to limit our electricity use because the electricity we demand is not derived from a nonrenewable source. So, the increased demand we place has no adverse effects on the planet, our neighbors, and our future generations.

Prevent Power Outages

We've all experienced this: when cooking or listening to the radio, the power suddenly goes out, and you have no idea when it will come back on. It can be aggravating to be without lights or working plugs for electrical appliances. The power outage could be caused by severe weather, which damages power lines and other electrical equipment used to supply electricity. Fortunately, off-grid solar systems enable us to store electricity in battery systems, guaranteeing that you never lose power or heat during blizzards or torrential downpours.

Reduce Electricity Costs Effectively

In many regions of the world, fossil fuels continue to be the main source of energy utilized to create power. Natural gas, petroleum, oil, and coal are some of the most commonly used fossil fuels. The cost of producing electricity using fossil fuels has risen over time as supply has become increasingly scarce. The cost of extracting these resources from the Earth has risen sharply. These rising costs have harmed consumers, as evidenced by the excessive utility bills that are due each month.

Installation is Simple

As more providers have entered the market and created cutting-edge technologies, the cost of the equipment needed to construct an off-grid solar power system has progressively declined over time. On the other hand, companies that provide installation services have raised their prices to capitalize on the growing demand of households ready to switch to solar power.

The Best Option for Remote Living

Access to electricity is a significant source of stress for people who live in remote areas prone to blackouts. A blackout is usually caused by a lack of proper electrical infrastructure to connect to the primary power grid. Investing in an off-grid solar power system will permanently remove this burden.

The independence from a utility company will save the household more money in the long run. Still, it will also provide the freedom to position the remote home in an open field, forest, or harbor. The remote home will become self-sufficient and have complete control over the amount of power used within the home.

Off-Grid Energy Solutions

Electric power and heating energy can be produced on-site with renewable energy sources such as solar (especially photovoltaic), wind, or micro-hydro. Alternative energy sources include biomass, usually coal, waste, and alcohol, and geothermal energy, which uses variations in ambient temperatures in daily indoor air conditions in buildings.

Electrical Energy

Grid-connected buildings generate electricity from power plants primarily using renewable fuels like coal and natural gas. The breakdown of global energy sources in 2017 reveals that the world uses the majority of non-renewables, with common renewables such as solar PV and wind electricity accounting for a small portion. Houses and households that are off-grid, such as in Africa, where 55% of residents do not have access to electricity, must take advantage of the green energy sources that support them, as they are the most accessible and self-sufficient.

Renewable Photovoltaic Electricity

Solar photovoltaics (PV) is one of the most common energy solutions for off-grid buildings because they use solar energy. PV arrays (solar panels) require converting solar energy into electrical energy. PV is affected by solar radiation as well as atmospheric temperature. Charge controllers, inverters, and fast shutdown controls are also required in a PV system.

Wind Generators

Another common source of off-grid electricity is wind energy, which wind turbines capture. Wind turbine components include blades propelled by the wind, gearboxes, regulators, engines, breakers, and roofs. The mechanical power obtained from the wind turbine is a measure of wind speed, air pressure, blade rotation, and the turbine's aerodynamic strength coefficient.

Microhydro

Hydropower is a potential energy solution where water is abundant. A dam and a reservoir are used in large-scale hydropower, while micro-hydro turbines can be used in rivers with constant water levels. Microhydro has the capacity to power homes and small communities, making it an excellent off-grid option. The volume of mechanical power generated is determined by a flow factor similar to that of wind turbines, the turbine's height, the velocity of the water, and the power coefficient. Energy from waves and tides will also be used to power coastal areas.

Batteries

When renewables produce electricity that is not immediately required, the energy is typically directed to charging a battery. This solves intermittent problems caused by intermittent renewable energy generation and allows for variations in building loads. Lead-acid and lithium-ion batteries are popular types of batteries.

Hybrid Power System

Many off-grid communities are developing hybrid energy systems to protect against intermittent problems and system failures. They mix conventional renewables, such as solar PV and wind, with more steady power sources, such as micro-hydro or diesel generators. This is more effective than extending networks to isolated communities.

Tips to Ensure a Successful Install

Installing your system is a distinct advantage, even better than any financial savings you may make. This is that you will have designed the system and know how it fits together and what to look at if any part needs to be replaced. This can be invaluable information if there is an issue with the system and it is impossible to contact assistance or get anyone to help for some time. This concern relates directly to why many consider off-grid or battery backup systems.

The following tips will help you to complete your installation successfully:

Preparation

Planning is one of the most important aspects of any project. Successful projects must always be planned and have a backup plan. When developing your strategy, keep the following points in mind:

A 3KW system will take approximately twenty-one square meters of space on your roof or a ground-mounted installation to power the average house. Before purchasing any panels, you should measure the available space. Ideally, you should have a larger space and the ability to expand your system in the future.

Fasteners are essential. Your choice of fasteners will determine where you intend to install the panels and the natural weather cycle in your area. If you live in an area prone to cyclones or tornadoes, you must ensure that your repair kit will likely withstand a cyclone or tornado; you do not want your installation ripped apart right before you need it.

Although many panels now offer comparable power production rates, the panels you choose and the inverter will affect the system's power generation and efficiency. While installing on a budget may entice you to select cheaper panels, you may find it more beneficial to select fewer panels of higher quality. Panels can always be added to your system.

Information

Solar energy remains a rapidly expanding and improving industry. Things that are at their best today may not be the same tomorrow. It is critical to keep up with technological advances because they will affect the prices of currently available solar panels or may even be worth waiting for if they offer significant advantages. Knowing the most recent research and techniques should also make installing your system more manageable.

Planning

You may notice a nearby house has solar panels; however, this does not automatically grant you the right to install solar panels on your property. Check with your local planning department and, if necessary, apply. You may also discover erecting them is acceptable, but there are restrictions on the quantity or some other minor stipulation. Knowing the planning regulations will help you avoid breaking them and having to remove your installation later.

Space

You've almost certainly thought about how much space you'll need to keep free for the solar panels. However, you might not have thought about where the ancillary parts will go. The inverter, batteries, and charge controller must all be located inside and easily accessible. You will also need to connect to your existing wiring. This could be as simple as connecting cables to the power supply of your fuse box, or it could require some new wiring. Whichever path you take, you will have to consider where the new wires are going; will they be fitted into the walls, out of sight? Knowing how much space is needed and where to find these items will make the installation process much easier.

Approval

Contact the utility company first to ensure a successful installation and determine their requirements. You can then ensure that you follow them; doing so will ensure that your new system is successful and has the potential to provide you with free power for the foreseeable future.

You will most likely find a dedicated section on their website where you can access information about their requirements and even fill out a form to get the paperwork side of the installation completed as soon as possible.

Installing your solar energy system is not only feasible; it is also relatively simple! All you need to do is a little planning and patience while designing the system and ensuring compliance with all relevant legalities.

1. Do Not Exceed 100 Amps

Always prioritize safety not only when it comes to protecting yourself but also when it comes to building safe solar systems. Numerous dangers and problems can occur when using an extremely high electrical current. A simple error in a highly charged system can be fatal or result in a property fire. Most solar charge controllers will instill a maximum of 80 amps for safety reasons, and deep cycle solar batteries will avoid providing a high current. It should be reassuring to know that your system components are regulated, but your responsibility is to exercise caution when using and wiring them.

2. Use the Highest Voltage Possible

Many people choose a 12-volt system because they believe it will be powerful enough to power their entire setup. When using 12 volts, however, you may notice a lot of voltage drops. Voltage drop is the loss of electrical power along the path of a current in an electrical circuit. Solar batteries don't usually provide a high current, and inverters have a specific voltage range they will operate within. As a result, if the battery bank voltage falls below a certain threshold, the inverter will simply shut down. The solution to this problem is to raise the system voltage from 12V-24V to 24V-48V.

3. Purchase the Thickest Wires You Can Afford

Investing in the largest and fattest wires you can afford is an additional strategy for lowering the likelihood of voltage drop. This is because heavier wires have less resistance than smaller and thinner wires. Having heavier and larger wires also allows you to carry heavier loads or upgrade your system in the future. This will allow you to prepare and prevent having to buy or replace extra cables in a year or two (unexpected costs are not fun).

4. Overbuild Rather than Underbuild Your System

When building an off-grid solar power system, numerous components, considerations, and processes exist. The accuracy in determining how much power you need in your home is crucial in building a functional system. It is too easy to overlook a calculation or certain figures, resulting in an underperforming system. As a result, I recommend adding at least 20% to 30% more solar panels and batteries than you had previously calculated to give your system room to grow if necessary.

5. Regularly Clean Your Panels

I always advise clients to install their solar arrays close to where they can access them frequently because they will need to do so on a regular basis. Our solar panels are frequently exposed to debris such as dirt, dust, pollen, bird droppings, and leaves, which if not regularly cleaned off, can reduce the power output of the solar panels. A rain shower will not do a great job cleaning the panels for you; you need to wash them daily. To wash panels, take a non-abrasive brush and warm soap water and gently clean and dry panels throughout the year.

Chapter 2: Off the Grid Living

Moving off the grid allows you to depend on solar power energy entirely. Cost-efficiency and a green lifestyle have made this concept highly accessible worldwide.

When thinking about moving off the grid, people ask several questions. The requirements and benefits are majorly associated with such questions. Here are all those questions answered:

How Much Energy Do I Need?

This question is valid, but the answer can vary depending on your energy needs. A medium-sized home requires about 900kWh of energy per month, but smartly installing solar panels can reduce this energy requirement.

Make a List of the Most Energy-Consuming Appliances

First, create a list that includes all the appliances consuming maximum energy on the grid. These can be:

- Air conditioner
- Lighting
- Refrigerator
- Electric furnace
- Clothes dryer
- Dishwasher
- Oven and others

Thanks to advanced solar panels, you can replace the energy source for all of these appliances, but it would be wise to eliminate those that are not so important in your household. This brings us to the next point.

Categorizing Loads that are Movable "Off-Grid"

You can get the energy to run the water heater, refrigerator, air conditioner, and other appliances, but it widely depends on how much energy you can generate in your area. The real point here is the capacity of solar panels, the available space for installation, and the sunlight exposure throughout the year. This will help you know the total amount of energy you can generate, and then you can decide which electric loads are more important to shift off the grid.

Make a List of Smaller Electrical Appliances

After evaluating your large loads, think about the overall smaller loads in your place. These loads can be small lights, computers, routers, and others. Although individually, they seem low energy consuming, an overall evaluation is essential.

Move to More Energy-Efficient Appliances

Before moving off the grid, it would be wise to design your home for solar power. This means you can choose energy-efficient appliances to re-design your household's energy consumption. Change the lighting, heating system, and other components where changes are possible.

You can even think about insulating your place as much as possible to gain maximum energy efficiency.

Can My Excess Energy Flow BACK to the Grid If I Want?

It is determined by your location and utility provider. Net metering is available in some areas. This method allows your excess energy to be fed back into the grid (if your solar system is connected to one), and you will receive credit for it.

However, some states do not allow net metering, which means you cannot choose to send excess energy back to the grid, so it is essential to check whether your state allows net metering.

Lower Monthly Energy Costs

Saving money on energy is probably the most significant benefit of using off-grid power. True, you must make some initial investments, but the installation is a one-time cost that saves you money on future monthly bills.

The savings will vary depending on your location, home size, energy requirements, and so on; however, installing solar panels can save you up to $100 per month. Most high-quality panels will last for more than 20 years, saving you an estimated $20,000 in most major cities.

Aside from that, if net metering is available in your state, you can use it. You can sell your excess energy to the utility grid and save money every month, but you must remain connected to the utility grid. Many believe that net metering is better than living entirely off the grid. This way, energy efficiency for the entire location is possible, saving you more monthly money.

Typically, net metering allows you to "sell" your excess energy to the grid as an energy credit. Then, when you need energy from the grid (due to low sunlight or extra energy demands), you don't have to pay for it. There are significant benefits to not going ultimately off the grid and instead using net metering.

Protection Against Blackouts

Blackouts are a common occurrence in many areas. If you live in such a location, an off-grid power source can come in handy. Your lights remain illuminated, ensuring the security and safety of your establishment. The solar power system will provide energy to the lights, allowing them to run continuously as you wish.

Even if blackouts are not a concern, you can relax about power availability. Grid power will be irrelevant.

Capability to Use for a Variety of Purposes

The variety of energy sources makes solar power more beneficial to everyone. Solar power generated by solar panels can be converted into electricity or heat. All you need is the right system. This allows you to run various appliances in your home or business without worrying about running out of power.

Low Upkeep is Required

Solar systems are well-known for requiring little maintenance. Simple cleaning is needed once or twice a year. Of course, this is dependent on the initial installation quality. You can also get solar panel cleaning at a reasonable price. Trusted manufacturers provide warranties for their panels, which allows you to avoid paying maintenance costs for an extended time. Whatever happens to your solar panels, your manufacturer will cover the costs.

Their upkeep determines the efficiency of the panels. This includes cable quality, as they transfer energy from one part to the next, so you should focus on getting your cables repaired regularly. This will not be too expensive compared to the savings from going off-grid.

Consistent Progress

Solar power is the future of energy consumption, with all major corporations investing in developing better technologies in this area. This means switching to solar energy allows you to get the most up-to-date power generation technology. The most recent technology gives you the best chance of utilizing power and energy.

As technology advances, you can upgrade your power system to achieve greater effectiveness and efficiency. Traditional grid energy does not provide this opportunity.

You now understand that moving from grid to solar power has distinct advantages. Understanding these advantages will aid you in making your final decision. Pay close attention to lifestyle quality and cost-cutting opportunities. You can have your energy supply and save all year.

Prepare yourself now that you've learned everything there is to know about solar power and solar panels. Select the best-suited panels, quality manufacturers, and utility providers if desired. Use what you've learned to make your daily power consumption more efficient and cost-effective. You can start by determining the exact amount of energy required and the cost associated with it. Afterward, proceed to the next step of locating and installing solar panels and other components.

Things to Consider Before Mounting a Solar Panel

- Consider the amount of power you need before deciding on an off-grid structure.
- What is the required battery storage for your solar system?
- Estimate the number of solar panels that can produce the required voltage.
- Choose a solar charge controller.
- Purchase an inverter for your solar system.
- There should be a balance of systems (BOS).

Surveying Your Site

You will also determine the output and size with the National Renewable Energy Laboratory (NREL). Of course, it is free to use.

The PVWatts calculator estimates the amount of electricity you can produce with a given solar system size by entering your home's location and several other factors. However, the PVWatts cannot help you measure the slope of your roof, the area you want to set up your solar, and your azimuth. You will have to measure these yourself.

Measuring Slope, Area, and Azimuth

These three values are the measurements that describe where the position and placement of your future solar panel would be. You will also need to have these values before using the PVWatts calculator.

Slope

The angle of your roof and the slope determines the tilt angle of the solar panel.

A roof slope is a relationship between a given roof plane's horizontal run and vertical rise. So, for example, if you have heard someone say (3:12) concerning roof slope, that means that the roof plane rises three inches over a twelve-inch level horizontal run. When measuring your roof's slope, it is vital to be as safe and accurate as possible.

You will need some tools to measure the roof slope:

- A ladder
- Level
- Tape measure
- Pencil

Here's how to go about measuring the roof slope based on the geometry of a right-angle triangle:

1. First, you need to get on top of your roof using a ladder.
2. If you have a roof with uneven planes (it doesn't have that flat pan to measure from), you will want to create a flat surface with something like a flat board that spans over the uneven areas to get an accurate reading.
3. With your pencil, mark a twelve-inch point on the level. (If your level is already twelve inches, you don't need to bother with this. It is only for people with a longer level).
4. After that, using your level, incline it from the start of the flat surface you created on the roof.
5. Next, measure from the twelve-inch mark on the level down to the roof surface using your tape.
6. Whatever ratio you get is your slope. (For example, if your tape measure reads three inches, your roof plane has a 3:12 slope).

7. Convert the rise-run slope you obtained to degrees. For instance, you can find conversion charts online at PVWatts (Tap on the 'i' in the 'tilt (deg)' row on the 'system info' page). You can also use a scientific calculator. You can obtain the degree angle by calculating the inverse tangent of the rise/run ratio. Simply divide the rising value by the run value and tap on the inverse tangent button on the calculator.

If you are putting your solar panel on the ground, you can use a level app on your smartphone. It may be part of the 'compass app.'

Area

Free space is available on your roof or ground for installing solar panels.

To get easy and accurate measurements, use a very long tape measure over twenty-five feet or longer. However, if you don't have a longer tape measure, you can take a piece of chalk to mark the roof at each measured distance. Although it might be frustrating and stressful, it will get the job done.

Here are the following steps to measure the available space on your rooftop:

1. Before climbing your rooftop to measure, take a few steps backward and draw a rough sketch of a simple area view map of any roof areas suitable for solar panels.
2. On the map, note the relative obstructions and penetration locations, such as chimneys, roof vents, satellite dishes, and plumbing pipes.
3. After this, you can now climb on the rooftop.
4. Measure the length and width of every roof plane on your map with your tape measure. A suitable space could measure at least twenty feet from the roof's ridge and twenty-five feet from side to side. (It is also possible to set up smaller groupings of solar panels in smaller areas on the roof).
5. From the installation area you measured, subtract over five to ten inches from each ridge and roof edge. The reason for subtracting is to leave a little space margin around the array.
6. Next, measure the exact locations of all obstacles and penetration and record them.

7. While measuring around all sides of each obstacle, including a margin of a few inches.
8. If an obstacle on the rooftop obstructs any installation area during the peak sun hours, you may need to omit the shaded area from your total.
9. Check with your local authorities before finalizing your roof layout plans.

For ground mount arrays, you need to measure the installation area on the ground on your property or yard.

Azimuth

This has to do with the particular directory that your ground mount or roof array faces. For example, west, south, north-west, etc., are measured in degrees.

How to measure azimuth:

1. A solar array facing due north possesses an azimuth of zero degrees.
2. A solar array facing due east has an azimuth of ninety degrees.
3. A solar array facing due south has an azimuth of one hundred and eighty degrees.
4. A solar array facing due west has an azimuth of two hundred and seventy degrees.
5. You can also measure your azimuth using a compass application on a smartphone or an old-fashioned compass.
6. Using smartphones is a lot easier. Why? Because your smartphone calibrates itself to your location, you don't have to account for magnetic declination.

To Use a Compass App:

1. Simply launch the compass app on your smartphone.
2. Follow the prompted instructions for calibration.
3. After configuring the compass app, stand with your back to the roof where the array will go.
4. Next, hold the phone flat in your hand and make sure it's directly in your front.

5. The compass application gives you the exact angle your roof plane faces. That angle is the azimuth of your roof.
6. You can make use of the old-fashioned compass the same way. Just make sure to consider the magnetic declination of your precise location.
7. If you plan on mounting your solar panel on the ground, it is best if the array faces due south (an azimuth of one hundred and eighty degrees).

Sizing Your System with PVWatts

Here's how to operate the PVWatts calculator to get the number of electricity you can produce per year:

1. Take a few minutes to go online to the PVWatts calculator. You can access this calculator on this site (https://www.pvwatts.nrel.gov).
2. Enter your home address, city, or state, then select 'Go.'
3. On the next page, tap on the map location closest to your house, or stick with your city's default location.
4. After, click on the big orange arrow labeled 'Go to system info.'
5. On the following page, tap on the big orange arrow labeled 'Go to PVWatts result.'
6. A number in a large type is displayed at the top. The number indicates how much A.C electricity you could produce per year at your location.

Easy right? No log-in registration is required, no unnecessary ads whatsoever, and most importantly, it is free! The system size and other default inputs are already inserted in the calculator.

PVWatts is presumptuously simple on the surface, but to improve your results' accuracy, there's much more you can do with it. The 'System Info' page is where you will enter your specific data for more accurate results. The PVWatts 'System Info' page comprises six basic design parameters for sizing your P.V. solar system. Let us briefly run through the features. (To see these tweaks, click on the 'i' button to the right of each parameter).

D.C. System Size

The system size is the rated D.C power output for the entire solar array. The default system size on PVWatts is (4 kW). You might use a solar panel array of (20 P.V.) panels rated (250 watts) for each panel. To get the total system size for the whole panel array combined, you must multiply (20 x 250 = 5000 watts = 5 kW). In this case, the default system size is (4 kW); you can decide to change the default system size to your calculated solar panel array's actual size.

Module Type

The module type parameter allows you to select one of the three types of P.V. solar panels you use for more accurate results. You can choose from standard, premium conventional, thin-film, or crystalline silicon (c-So) modules.

Array Type

This is where you select the solar panel-mounting type you use —rooftop mount, ground mount, *etc.* Whichever one you are using, just select it.

System Losses

This is the total of all the small reductions in efficiency due to real-world operating conditions and equipment inefficiencies. Due to these factors, the actual D.C power received from the sun cannot equal the amount of A.C power sent into your house.

Tilt

Tilt is the angle of your P.V. solar panels, measured in degrees.

Azimuth

Once you adjust all these parameters, navigate to the 'System Info' page, and tap on the orange arrow labeled 'Go to PVWatts results.' After inputting more accurate results, the number you get is the average annual kilo-watt-hour production you can expect with a (5

K.W.) system. (unless you entered a different system size, you might get a different result from a (5 K.W.) system).

Snow

Solar panels don't produce a lot of electricity when covered in snow. When snow falls, the sky is cloudy; with that alone, power is produced.

A solar panel covered in snow makes things more challenging. If you want to speed up the process of getting snow off the panels, use a wood-handle broom or mop that won't scratch the glass of the solar panels.

Once you clear the snow or it melts away and the sun starts to shine again, the solar panel receives a lot of power from the sun once more.

Mistakes You Should Avoid When Installing An Off-Grid Solar Power

Inadequate Solar System Sizing

The most common mistake is incorrectly sizing a solar power system. It frequently results from mental heuristics and basing power requirements on variables that are inaccurate representations of how much power is consumed. For instance, you might believe that you use X amount of power based on your most recent utility bill but in fact this number varies with the seasons. Other factors must be considered when deciding on power usage, such as changing climate temperatures, panel positioning, and efficiency.

Renting Out Your System

Only if you own the system are solar power systems a good investment. There are numerous disadvantages to leasing a solar system. To begin, the region provides tax breaks for installing solar systems in homes; however, you would not receive these if you leased your system (they would go toward the actual owner). Second, while leasing may appear more affordable monthly, you will pay excessive interest. It would also bind you to contracts that directly contradict your self-sufficient lifestyle. As a result, I recommend you buy your system and give yourself the peace of mind you deserve.

Not Planning Ahead

When many people decide to build an off-grid solar power system, they mistake calculating how much power they use now and failing to consider how it will be used in future homes.

Purchasing Low-cost Solar Panels Attempting to Save Money

I completely understand why a low-cost solar panel would appeal to any customer (I love a good discount too). However, you must know when to distinguish between a discount and a low-quality solar panel being thrown into the market. Because of the increased demand for solar power, there have been some new entrants, with many offering systems made in China at exorbitant prices.

Ignoring the Warranty Terms

In the solar sector, the length of a product's warranty is believed to be closely tied to the manufacturer's faith in its product. In other words, it is assumed that the product is of poor quality and performs poorly when the guarantee duration is limited. When shopping for solar products, keep this in mind and look for products that will last the longest. Understand the warranty's terms and the services it covers. Please do not be misled by performance warranties that promise the industry-wide lifespan of a product. Look for a manufacturer's warranty, which should last about ten years.

Sun-tracking Systems are Used

Many believe that sun-tracking systems will help them increase the amount of energy produced by their solar panel array. On the other hand, purchasing a sun tracking system may be another expense on an ever-expanding list. This is because investing in more solar panels and proactively addressing your need for increased energy production would be preferable to buying a tracker (which may or may not help "track" more sunlight). Furthermore, sun-tracking systems are susceptible to system failures, so don't expect them to last as long as your solar panels.

Choosing Not to Buy a Battery Monitor

Battery monitors are useful tools that offer crucial details about the condition and health of the battery bank. This device aids in the upkeep of the bank by detecting problems with the off-grid solar power system or current levels of power available. This information is especially beneficial to those still learning about solar power and require as much assistance in understanding their solar power system as possible. Furthermore, the battery monitor will measure and track the total amp hours accumulated in the system, allowing you to monitor a household's energy usage.

Not Upgrading to More Energy-Efficient Appliances

The last thing you want to happen after you have a fully functional off-grid solar power system is energy misuse or waste. You waste energy when you use appliances that consume a lot of unnecessary energy. You may reduce your energy use while still enjoying the benefits of utilizing electronic gadgets and appliances by altering your living habits and choosing more energy-efficient appliances. A simple lifestyle change can save significant energy, such as switching to LED light bulbs instead of incandescent ones.

Not Purchasing a Backup Generator

Generators may appear to be an unnecessary expense when installing an off-grid solar power system. Still, they are an essential system component, especially if you have decided to go entirely off the grid. One of the primary reasons people choose to go off-grid is to have the freedom to power their homes however they see fit. You cannot control unpredictable weather conditions, but you can plan for them. Your generator will come in handy in the event of a disaster, which can occur at any time. When designing your off-grid solar power system, you cannot assume that the climate will always be consistent and neutral.

Failure to Keep Up with New Technology

Since the solar power sector is still relatively young, new updates and products are constantly being produced. This is good news for you because you are always presented with opportunities to make the solar power system more efficient. It also means that owning a solar system is becoming more affordable because of the demand for solar products. Keeping up to date with new technologies will help you purchase more efficient components, creating an overall efficient solar power system. It will also expose you to more environmentally friendly alternatives to building a solar power system, reducing your overall carbon footprint.

BOOK 2

Chapter 3: Necessary Equipment for Installing Off-Grid Solar Systems

Solar power systems can last for decades if they are well-connected. Installing solar power systems can be easy if you have the essential components.

Some of the necessary equipment for mounting a solid off-grid solar system includes:

Backup Generator

Backup generators help prevent blackouts if there is no sunshine over the area for some days. Installing a gasoline backup generator is preferred over a large battery bank. This later may not be efficient if the occasion demands that.

Most backup generators can function with fuel, propane, and gasoline. The primary output of the generating set is alternating current. This current goes through the inverter system to become a direct current for immediate use. It could also be stored in the battery storage as Dc for future use.

Solar Performance Monitor

The solar performance monitor will show how much electricity is generated per hour, day, and year. This is to verify the performance of the photovoltaic system. This monitoring system can also detect potential performance changes. This tool must confirm if your particular solar power system is operating at its best. You can even detect problems before they become a significant issue.

The solar performance monitor operates through the inverters. As your inverter converts direct current to alternating current, information about the power levels and production is sent to various cloud-based monitoring systems. Homeowners can then access this information through a smart device or mobile app. It's incredible how we have been able to control the sun to a degree through the internet.

A system with a power optimizer won't rely on a wireless connection to transmit data. Therefore, you can continue to monitor your system if there is an internet outage.

DC Connects

Every solar power installation requires AC and DC safety disconnects. These features are attached between the inverter and battery bank. It helps switch the current flow between the two major solar system components. DC connects help prevent electrical fires, troubleshoot, and maintain the device.

Inverters

You may not need an inverter if the solar system is for powering your vehicles or a small apartment that operates with a direct current. But you may use an inverter to convert direct current to alternating current for all electrical appliances.

Unlike on-grid inverters, inverters for off-grid solar systems don't match phase with utility sine waves. Current moves through the solar charge controller from the solar panels. The solar power bank banks the current before the inverter transforms it into an alternating current.

When electrical power generation became commercial at the beginning of the 20th century, power plants would produce vast amounts of DC power but quickly discovered that it couldn't be transmitted efficiently over long distances. This limited the coverage area that power plants had. In addition, the more power plants could generate, the more that got lost in transmission.

Initially, this made electrical power unviable until Nikola Tesla discovered Alternate Current (AC). Eventually, Tesla's idea became commercially viable, and electrical power consumption spread widely around the globe.

Since then, virtually all appliances have been powered by AC, the type of energy used for residential customers. Moreover, smaller electronic devices such as cell phones and laptops run on DC. Cell phones and laptop chargers have a built-in converter that converts AC into DC so that these devices can run. Other batteries, such as the run-of-the-the-mill Duracell and Energizer kind, also produce DC. The chemical reaction within the battery generates a given amount of voltage and current, which powers devices.

So, after a brief physics class and some history, you can see why the inverter is necessary.

Types of Inverter Technology for Solar Systems

String Inverters

These are used to connect panels. Numerous stringing configurations will influence how each system performs. These inverters are designed to work with panels that are strung together. When multiple panels are connected in this manner, the output is dependent on the performance of the worst-performing solar panel. As a result, if one of them is shaded, the entire set is affected. This won't be a problem if your roof has a lot of southern exposure. String inverters have the advantage of being the most affordable. String inverters are mounted on a wall in a shaded area. This can convert solar energy from a string of panels into alternating current. This type of electric current is appropriate for both businesses and homes.

In a string inverter system, if a shadow or partial darkness covers any part of the panel, it usually affects the functionality of other parts of the solar panel. This issue, however, can be overcome with microinverters. They allow the panels to operate separately and independently of one another. Their prices, however, are higher than those of other types of inverters.

Power optimizers are a type of intermediate device. This system aids in the transition between the two types of inverters. However, it is less effective and less expensive than the other type. Power optimizers are unaffected by shading. As a result, microinverters are not required.

Microinverters

At the back of each panel in the system, these types of inverters convert direct current to alternating current. This eliminates the issue of having a few panels that are harmed by shade. Maximum alternating current shifts from the solar panel into your home and the primary grid are achieved even in shady conditions. Microinverters increased efficiency by 27% in partially shaded installations, according to research conducted at the University of Virginia. An inverter on each panel allows for monitoring unexpected performance issues.

Solar micro-inverters are more expensive than string inverters but facilitate system expansion.

Power Optimizers

These are attached to the back of each solar panel in the same way that microinverters are. This, once again, enables individual panel monitoring. The difference is that they do not convert direct current to alternating current. They monitor the voltage of the direct current flowing through the strings of the solar array to ensure that the maximum amount of power is sent to the inverter. The optimized direct current is then converted to alternating current by a smaller inverter. Battery backup systems benefit greatly from power optimizers. These systems are more efficient and less expensive than microinverters. The power from your solar panels can directly charge the battery, avoiding system losses caused by conversion from direct to alternating current and back again.

Hybrid inverters work well with home battery backup systems as well. They can convert direct current from solar panels to alternating current for your home and alternating current from the grid to direct current for charging your battery bank.

Charge controllers on hybrid inverters detect when to direct solar energy to your home, the grid, or the battery. It can also detect when to draw electricity from the primary grid and store it in the battery. Many hybrid inverters are less expensive in the beginning.

Solar inverters are why the electricity from your solar panels becomes usable in your home. Get multiple estimates to determine which kind of inverter is best for you.

Other Inverters

Square Wave Inverter

This type of inverter derives its name from the type of wave it generates. When visualized, the wave it makes looks like squares instead of curves. Square wave inverters are good at powering simple tools with universal motors. But I don't recommend it to use with other things. This type of inverter is rarely used nowadays and is not the safest choice for your appliances.

Pure Sine Wave Inverters

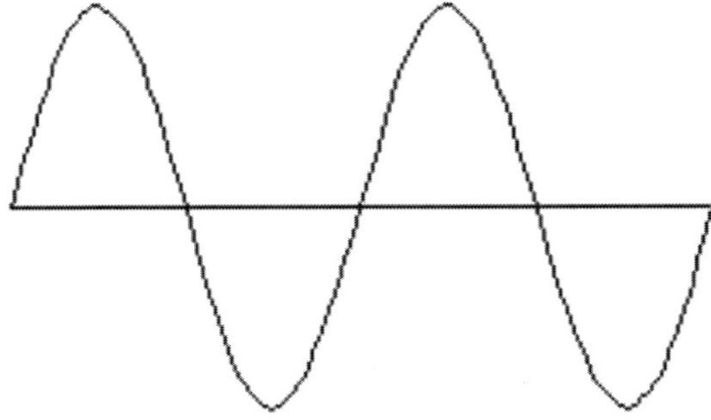

These types of inverters are the most efficient of their kind. This is because they bear the closest resemblance to pure AC.

Since the pure sine wave inverter is the one that closest resembles the pure AC wave, it is a lot more efficient and is safe to use for your appliances.

Modified Sine Wave Inverter

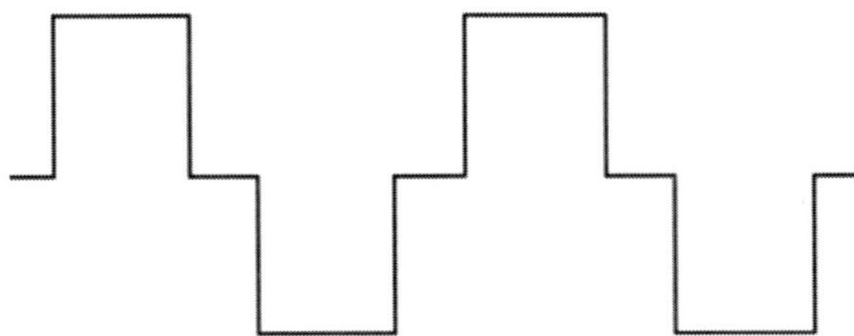

This type of inverter seems to be between a square wave inverter and a pure sine wave inverter.

The reason for their existence is due to cost. Since there are folks who cannot afford a pure sine wave inverter but want something better than a square wave one, they can choose a modified sine wave inverter.

Personally, modified sine wave inverters are a good option for smaller systems, such as in a small home or a cabin. A modified sine wave inverter may be a good option if you want to power a tiny home or an RV on pure solar power.

I would not advise purchasing a modified sine wave inverter if you can afford a pure sine wave inverter.

There is a list of appliances you can't use with a modified sine wave inverter, for example, medical equipment, laser printers, photocopiers, laptops, devices with microprocessor controllers, home automation systems, and more.

The grid communication function ensures that no solar panel power makes it outside your home in the event of a temporary power outage. This prevents line workers who are troubleshooting outside from getting zapped. The inverter will also feed power loads into the grid when your home does not need power and the battery is full. This is if the grid is connected to your solar power system.

Inverters will shut down for safety when a hazardous electrical arc is detected caused by system aging and material degradation.

Calculating The Size Of An Inverter

We can calculate the size of an inverter needed for our system just by summing all appliances load (watts) that we will be using at once:

For example:

Let's assume you are powering a few light bulbs (50 watts), a television (100), a refrigerator (300 watts), charging phones and laptops (100 watts), and running a fan (50 watts), microwave (700 watts).

Now let's sum up:

Pmax = 50+100+300+100+50+700= 1300 watts

Now we must determine the capacity of our off-grid inverter; if no power losses occur during the conversion of DC power to AC power, our calculated maximum load could be the inverter capacity.

But, since no power conversion is completely efficient (heating losses exist), we must know how efficient the inverter we will use is.

Assume that our inverter has a 90% efficiency.

As a result, we can calculate the required solar inverter power rating or capacity as follows:

1300 watts / 0.90 = 1444,4 watts Pmax / Inverter efficiency

In this case, we will need to purchase at least a 1500-watt inverter because 1444-watt inverters are unavailable.

Whether you select a pure sine wave or a modified sine wave inverter, you must ensure that it can handle the maximum load for your system (1300 watts).

Doesn't that seem straightforward?

Remember that a pure sine wave inverter may produce up to 95% of the total maximum load. As a result, if you produce 100 watts, your system's net power will be 95 watts. If you're using a square wave inverter, you should expect to get around 90% of your total output. While that may not appear to be much on the surface, you may encounter problems if you go full-throttle on the system.

So, if your maximum load is 1300, it is always better to choose a ten or even 20% larger inverter just to be safe. At least 1444 watts in our case. 1500-watt inverters are available for purchase.

Another crucial consideration. If you have a 12-volt system, you must consider this when looking at the specifications of the inverter you choose. So, if you have a 12-volt system, you may need a 12-volt DC to 230/220 volts 50 Hz inverter (if you live in Europe) or a 120 volts 60 Hz inverter (USA).

Keep in mind that the inverter must be logically related to the voltage of your batteries. Your inverter should reflect this voltage if you have 24-volt or 48-volt systems.

Some appliances, such as hairdryers, vacuum cleaners, and washing machines, consume significant power before returning to their average power consumption. As a result, you must consider this when calculating your maximum load. Check the start-up wattage for these appliances and use these numbers to calculate your maximum load; you may need a much larger inverter.

Choosing An Inverter

We will require a 2000-watt battery inverter for most mobile solar power systems.

For stationary solar power systems, it will be much more than 2000-watt inverters (because we might want to use many appliances at once).

Almost all inductive loads like hoovers, motors, and microwaves initially required much more power than working power to start work. For example, if you use a 1200-watt inverter to power a 1200-watt hoover, it will most likely not work because the initial power that the hoover needs is about 2000 watts. So, for running a hoover, you will probably need at least a 2000-watt inverter.

If we choose an inverter that's too small, it can fail by working too hard to power the appliances we will constantly use.

We need to choose between 2 types of inverters:

- MSW (modified sine wave) inverters (cheaper)
- TSW (true sine inverters) or often called a pure sine inverter: TSW is safer to use with sensitive appliances such as monitors or computers, produces less noise, MSW produces buzzing when working, and audio equipment can buzz even more.

Inductive loads run more efficiently when you power them with a pure sine wave inverter.

This is the hardest working piece of equipment in the solar power system. Its main function is to convert the direct current flowing from the solar panels into an alternating current for your home. The other functions of the inverter include:

- Voltage tracking
- Grid communication
- Emergency shutoff

For the voltage tracking function, the inverters will continually track the solar array's voltage to determine the maximum power at which the solar panels will work. This will ensure the system always creates the most power. You will need two different inverters for grid-tied and off-grid systems.

Solar Charge Controllers

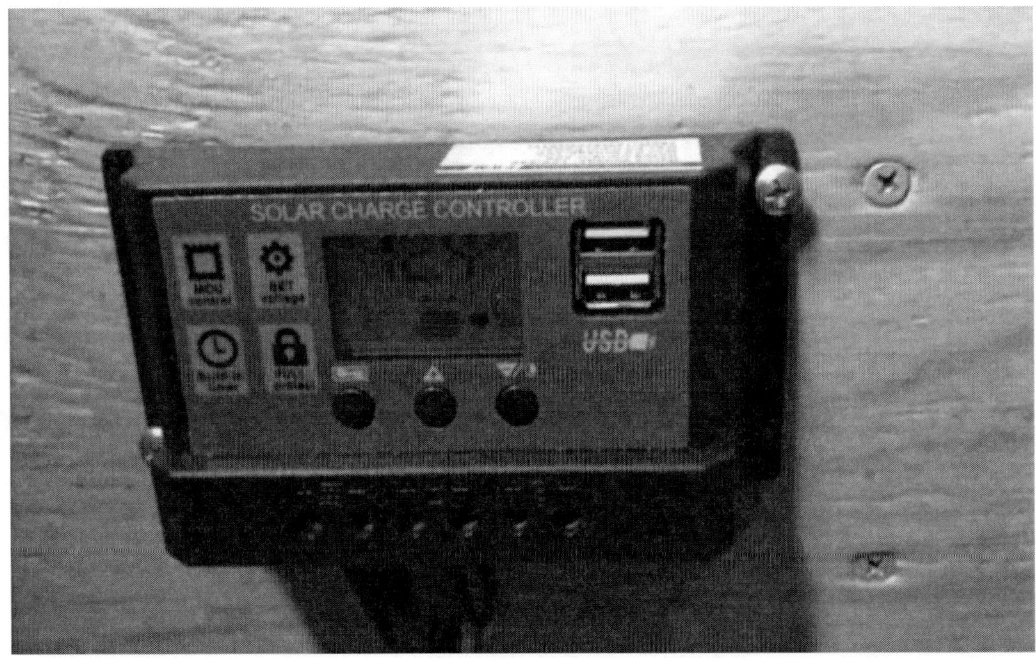

Solar charge controllers are known as battery regulators or charge regulators. It helps to manage the battery life of your solar array. Charge controllers prevent much current from flowing into the system and damaging the unit. It also protects the batteries from overcharging. Most charge controllers are integrated with the inverter system of the solar plant.

On your journey to setting up a functioning off-grid solar system, you will need to get a solar charge controller, be familiar with all its components, and connect it to your solar panel and your battery, so let's get started.

A charge controller's basic function is to regulate the supply of power coming from the solar panel into your battery to keep it from overcharging or passing its DOD level.

So, getting a solar charge controller is not an option for you - it's a necessity! Except you want to spend money getting new batteries every month (overcharging can spoil your battery).

Here are the following displays that you see on your solar charge controller screen.

Main Display

This feature displays for you whether your solar panel is or is not charging your battery (the icon on the extreme left side), what level your battery is at (the icon in the middle), and the load (the bulb-looking icon).

You can always turn the load on or off if you want it to stop draining your battery. It also displays the battery's current voltage (the large number on the screen with 'V' for voltage).

If your solar panel isn't charging your battery, the panel icon will not be displayed on the screen. If your load (bulb icon) isn't displayed on the screen, it means your load is not draining any power from your battery.

Float Voltage Display

This feature usually comes with a default value of (13.7 volts). However, you can always re-configure it. It is the voltage at which you want your battery to stay.

Discharge Stop Display

When there is a load on your solar charge controller, it's pulling a lot of power. You can set a fixed minimum voltage with your solar charge controller (10.7 volts).

So, as your load is draining power from your battery, the instant your battery reaches the fixed minimum voltage (10.7 volts). You set it, and the charge controller automatically disconnects your load from further draining your battery.

Discharge Reconnect Display

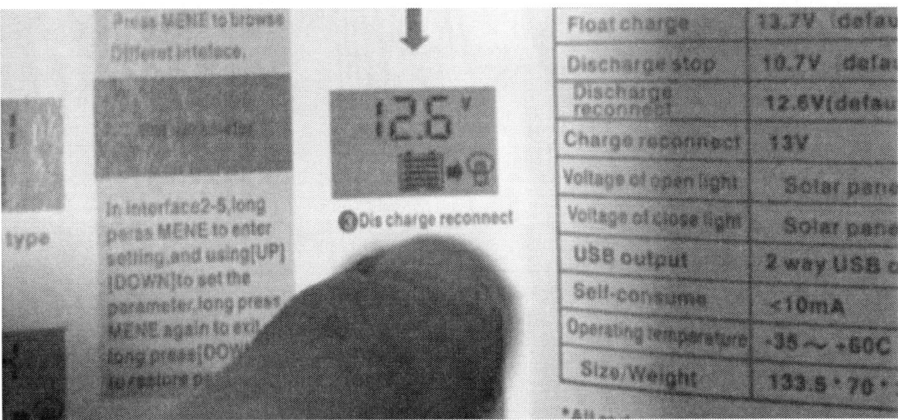

You can set this feature to a fixed voltage.

For example, if you put the discharge reconnect value at 12.6 volts, once your battery starts charging with your solar panel and reaches the discharge reconnect value (12.6 volts), it automatically allows your battery to start powering your load back again.

Work Mode Display

With this feature, you can set how many hours your load will be used in a day.

Note: All the values mentioned are default; you can always customize them to meet your various needs.

Connecting your Solar Panel to Your Solar Charge Controller

The bottom side of your solar charge controller are holes for different connections.

On some charge controllers, they would indicate where your positive and negative wire will go into.

How to connect them:

1. After you've set up your solar panel, it should have positive and negative output wires.
2. On your solar charge controller, the would have holes on the bottom end of the device where the positive and negative wires will go.
3. The first two holes are for connecting the solar panel with the charge controller.
4. The solar panel's positive and negative wires will go into the charge controller indicated on the device's bottom side.
5. You will need your screwdriver to unscrew the bolt in the hole to put the wires inside the holes. Insert your positive solar wire into the positive terminal and your solar panel negative wire into the negative terminal. Then, screw the bolt back in to hold the wire firmly.

How to Connect Your Solar Charge Controller to Your Solar Battery

This is quite similar to the solar panel-charge controller connection.

1. Get two lead wires of opposite polarities (positive and negative).

2. Insert them into the two holes in the solar charge controller reserved for battery connection.
3. Using a screwdriver, unscrew the bolts, and insert the right wire into the right hole (positive wire for a positive hole and negative wire into the negative hole).
4. Screw back the bolts to hold the wire firm.
5. Next, you must connect the wires to your battery's positive and negative terminals.
6. With your hand, slightly unscrew the terminal bolt of the battery a little bit, hook, or wrap your wire around the terminal screw and screw it back to hold the wire firmly.
7. Do this for the positive and negative wires.
8. Once you've done that, you will notice that your charge controller has powered on automatically.

Solar Charge Controller Tips

On the control panel of the charge controller, there are led lights indicating temperature, power from the solar panel, and battery.

The led light for power from the solar panel displays two patterns of light:

- A steady green light from the led bulb means charging.
- Blinking green light means over-voltage.

The led light for battery displays:

- A blinking green light meaning the battery is full
- A steady green light meaning the battery is normal
- An orange blinking light for a low battery
- A red light for a depleted battery

Charge Controller to Batteries

Since the Battery Bank spot can get very hot, you will need wires that can withstand higher temperatures. Therefore, I recommend you use a HH wire type, like THHN-2.

Moreover, Batteries are made of chemicals, so you can also consider XHHW-2 wires for extra safety. When they fail, lead-acid batteries also produce water, so a water-resistant wire is always a good idea.

Again, choose a water-resistant wire on boats and in wet conditions.

As per the Current needs, keep the same gauge and diameter of the wires coming from the Combiner Box.

Batteries to Batteries

We're still talking about Batteries, so the same recommendations are valid here. Use a wire type with high heat, water, and chemical resistance.

As the Batteries will be connected to the Inverter, which is connected to the loads, we can safely presume that higher Current demand will happen sooner or later. I suggest you use even thicker cables, ranging from 3 to 3/0 AWG.

When connecting multiple Batteries, use wires of the same length, diameter/AWG, and from the same manufacturer.

Batteries to Inverter

Same as above. We are still in the Battery Bank's case.

Inverter to Loads

Apart from boats and very wet environments, we can safely state that there are dry conditions inside the living space of your camper truck or cabin. Therefore THHN-2 cables are more than enough.

Here a smaller diameter wire suffices, too. You can safely choose a 12-14 AWG gauge.

Fuses

Fuses are essential to protect your circuit from overheating, melting, and even catching fire. Not all fuses are equal, though. Fuse sizes must be based on the wire size you connect them to.

Fuse size for solar panel wires is often indicated on the datasheet.

Remember to place the fuses on the red (positive) wire close to the energy source.

Shunts

A shunt is a current resistor or ammeter. A high-precision resistor enables us to measure Voltage and Current by dividing the input Voltage by the shunt's resistance (thank you, Mr. Ohm). Shunts must be connected in series on the DC line to do so.

Voltage, Current, Resistance. That's a bunch of useful data, right?

Precisely! And that is why, in PV systems, you often use shunts with Battery Monitors to get accurate readings of Current, Voltage, State of Charge, and stuff.

How to choose a shunt?

First, the maximum Current that the shunt can bear has to match the Current coming out from your Battery Bank.

Second, if you are using a shunt to pair it with a Battery Monitor, as it most likely is, the shunt has to match its specs, too.

Note: don't use a shunt with a higher rating than the load since the measurement will be inaccurate.

Batteries

Choosing the right batteries for your solar system is very important. Why? Because you are using an off-grid solar system, the sun's energy supplied to the solar panel cannot be used directly because the energy varies. Sometimes it might supply full energy, and sometimes the energy supply may be low due to cloudy weather.

The essence of batteries in an off-grid solar system is to provide a constant power source for your electrical appliances, whether on a cloudy or sunny day. Knowing this, you cannot afford to get a bad or faulty battery that won't serve your needs. Also, choosing a battery depends on what you are planning on powering. If you are used to appliances with heavy loads, you cannot afford to get a battery with a smaller capacity.

Types of Batteries

Various batteries are available for your solar panel installations. These include lead-acid batteries, lithium-ion batteries, and saltwater batteries.

Batteries Made of Lithium-ion

Lithium-ion batteries are the latest technology in modern appliances. Lithium-ion batteries can be used in solar power systems. They are more compact, lightweight, and long-lasting. Some of the advantages of this type of battery include its longer lifespan and high rate of depth of discharge (DoD).

Lithium-ion batteries are more expensive than other kinds of batteries. You can choose a low-cost battery for your solar systems.

These are the batteries found in laptops and iPhones. With 4,000-6,000 cycles, these batteries outlast lead-acid batteries. They also have an 80% discharge capacity. As a result, they typically last 13-18 years. The main disadvantage is that they are approximately 50% more expensive than lead batteries.

Batteries Made of Saltwater

Saltwater batteries are the most recent industry options. They contain no heavy metals and are not bulky. These batteries make use of electrolytes that contain saltwater. Because they are renewable and easy to dispose of, this is one of the best batteries for green energy technologies. This is in contrast to lithium-ion and lead-acid batteries, which must be disposed of properly to avoid contaminating the environment. This battery is a new technology that has not been thoroughly tested.

Batteries Made of Lead-Acid

Lead-acid batteries have long been the best backup and power bank for your energy grid system. Compared to other types of batteries, these have a lower depth of discharge (DoD) and a shorter lifespan.

Lead-acid batteries are reasonably priced. If you have a large array of solar panels, you can use them. They are, once again, the best for off-grid solar power users.

These are some of the oldest and most reliable types of batteries. Depending on how frequently you discharge them, these batteries can last anywhere from two to eight years.

Their cycle life ranges from 1000 to 3000. If you choose these batteries, keeping them in a shed away from the heat is best. Heat can significantly reduce the lifespan of these batteries. These batteries have a discharge capacity of 60%, which means you can only use 60% of their ability. Any longer, the battery degrades much faster.

Flow

A flow battery comprises a water-based solution called zinc bromide that flows between two tanks. During charging, zinc is extracted from the liquid and stored separately. During discharge, the zinc is put back into the liquid. The zinc flows from the big plastic at the bottom to the electrodes on the top. These batteries have 100% discharge capacity, which does not affect the battery's lifespan. The following are a few more advantages:

- They can withstand a high level of heat.
- The zinc-bromide solution is a natural fire retardant.
- Because of the physical separation of the battery's components, there is no chance of an explosion.
- They can sit on a shelf without being charged and not degrade.

The main disadvantage is that they have a maximum lifespan of about 4,000 cycles, slightly less than lithium-ion batteries, on average.

Sodium Nickel Chloride

These batteries have a broad operating temperature range between negative 4-Degrees Fahrenheit and 140-Degrees Fahrenheit. They are also fully rechargeable with no toxic or dangerous chemicals. Finally, there is no fire risk due to the battery's chemistry.

The main disadvantage is that the expected lifespan is about 3,500 cycles at 80% discharge capacity. These batteries are also much more expensive than lithium-ion batteries, running about $20,000 installed.

Battery Lifespan

The whole point of having a home energy storage battery is to use it and charge it on and on. This cycle continues! It is no news that batteries cannot last forever, although they might last very long depending on the type of battery you are using. Eventually, they will die. Let's compare a solar battery to your phone's battery.

Once you fully charge your phone battery, you use up the battery and recharge it again. Eventually, after some years, you will notice that your battery doesn't hold up as much as it used to. This is the same for solar batteries.

Now, the question is, how long will your solar battery last?

There's no general answer to this question as it depends solely on your battery. However, with proper maintenance, your battery could last longer!

You may consider including battery technology in your solar array if you need to use the system at night. Also, you should consider the rate of feed-in tariffs. The government pays you for sending back the electrical energy you generated into the common power grid available for everyone. This payment is called the feed-in tariffs.

In that vein, excess energy stored in your power bank or batteries is not being paid for since you are not sending it out to the communal grid. You may consider using battery technology if the authorities offer a high feed-in tariff (FIT).

Another suitable name for solar power batteries is deep cycle batteries—this battery stores renewable energy from the sun, wind, and other green energy forms. Off-grid solar systems require solar batteries as a power bank. It is used for storing excess energy from the power station and could serve as a backup in case of power failure in the grid.

Solar batteries enable you to have light if the sun is down or if there is a power outage from the grid. These batteries are designed to be discharged during power consumption and recharged to store excess energy during sun peak hours.

You can maintain your batteries' life by limiting the discharge rate. This is called depth of discharge (DOD) and should be limited to at least twenty percent. Most inverters have low voltage disconnect characteristics. This enables the system to disconnect excess loads at a specific time. Solar batteries have a state of charge, which should be eighty percent or greater. But it is advisable to maintain a minimal discharge limit of fifty percent.

Solar batteries have low voltage alarms to give you a warning when the battery is low. Other devices that can help you check your battery's health with accurate statistics of your system's performance are voltmeters, battery monitors, and ammeters.

Estimating Battery Bank Sizes

Allowing your solar batteries to discharge to an unhealthy point is not ideal for your PV system. You should consider the battery bank size if you purchase a solar array for your small apartments, RVs, vans, and vehicles. This consideration is necessary to select a suitable battery that can carry the loads in your home and vehicles.

You can create a battery bank by interconnecting several batteries with different wiring systems. This will help you to get the right battery bank size for your solar array.

Factors to Consider Before Choosing the Right Battery Size

Budget

How much money did you set aside for your solar battery bank? Understanding how many batteries you can buy conveniently for the project is critical. Again, your money will determine whether you purchase a superior battery, such as lithium-ion or lead-acid batteries, which can last longer for your solar grid.

Determine the Load you Want to Connect

How many appliances or equipment can you connect to the power grid? This will determine the amount of load your solar system can handle and the power required to keep your apartment active and electrified. This thought will help you determine how many batteries to connect to your solar arrays. Make sure your solar arrays outnumber your battery bank. This is required to compensate for power loss caused by system aging and wear. Mitigating the effects of power fluctuations and voltage drops is also necessary.

Check the Voltage of Your Solar Power System

Another factor that determines the size of your battery bank is the voltage your solar system can generate. If your solar panel can generate 50 volts, make sure your battery bank can also store 50 volts. However, having a battery bank with less voltage storage is preferable in the event of a sudden voltage drop. A battery bank with a power storage capacity of 30 volts can be linked to a solar power system generating 40 volts.

The Storage Capacity

Before sizing your solar power station, check the battery bank's storage capacity. If you get less sunlight during the day, you'll need more battery banks to store more energy at night. The more power you have stored, the more loads your solar system can support.

Consider Days of Autonomy

After fully charging your battery bank, you may want to take some days off without charging the battery. These are referred to as autonomy days. This is an important consideration when sizing your battery bank. This is because the more you recharge the batteries, the more they run down, and their lifespan decreases.

Determine the Depth of Discharge (DoD)

The level of discharge you want your battery to reach before it needs to be recharged. This is determined by the demand for electricity in your area. Another consideration is the battery's capacity. All of these factors work together to shorten the battery's lifespan.

The Rate of Discharge

The discharge rate in your batteries will affect how many hours or days you can go without a recharge, especially if there is less sunlight in the area. Slower discharge rate batteries can carry more loads and last longer.

Look for a battery's (C-) sign to determine its discharge rate. A battery with (C-5) on it can take up to five hours to completely discharge.

Use a Higher Voltage Power Generator

Depending on the sunlight available in your area to recharge the solar system through the panels, you can also use an alternative generating set to recharge the batteries and power your devices. Some photovoltaic modules are designed for peak power points ranging from 16 to 18 volts. If the voltage falls below 5%, the charge current in the battery will be affected, as will the voltage.

Panels

The panels are the most important part of any solar system. They are responsible for absorbing the sun's energy. They will then convert the photons, or energy particles in light, into usable electricity to power electrical loads. These panels can be used in various settings, including remote locations such as cabins and residential and commercial buildings.

Individual solar cells, which are made up of many layers of silicon, phosphorus, and boron, make up solar panels. Phosphorus provides a slightly negative charge, while boron provides the slightly positive charge required for the reactions. These lengthy and complicated reactions are referred to as the Photovoltaic Effect, which was discussed earlier in this book.

The average house has more than enough roof space to accommodate the required number of panels. While the sun is shining, the panels will generate more than enough energy to power the hoe. The excess energy produced will be fed into the home's primary power grid and used for electricity at night.

Solar panels are a very efficient way to produce electricity for various applications. Many people who want to live off the grid love producing solar power through this method because they don't have to rely on anyone else but the good old sun to provide them with energy.

Solar Panels in a Field

This is often done for shared or community solar energy resources.

The panels are the part of the system you can see on the roofs or walls. The panels have built-in solar cells. As the sunlight hits the panels, the electrons are stimulated to flow through the solar cells. The radiation from the sun's rays helps to produce electricity. It is light from the sun that produces electricity and not heat energy.

When the panels are overheated, they could become inefficient in generating the desired current. Therefore, ensure that your chosen solar panel is strong to resist harsh weather conditions. Varieties of solar panels are on the market. Here are some features of good solar panels for your cars, RVs, boats, vans, and small homes.

Types of Panels

Different types of solar panels are on the market. We have monocrystalline panels and polycrystalline panels. These types of panels are darker in color. They are made with singular large crystals.

- Polycrystalline panels are usually dark blue or light in color. The textures vary with some lighter patches. They consist of multiple smaller crystals.
- Monocrystalline panels are superior to others on the market. They also generate higher frequency currents than others. The reason is that large crystal balls absorb greater radiation from sunlight.

Rigid Solar Panels

Rigid solar panels come in various designs, from large panels for big residential apartments to smaller panels of 50 watts capacity to charge a few appliances. These photovoltaic panels are installed on aluminum frames. They are made for outdoor use and often mounted under tempered glass.

These rigid solar panels could withstand wind, hailstones, and sand. It is designed for long-term use and is highly efficient. The panel is resistant to scratches and can withstand an ice scraper.

Common rigid panels are designed with less wattage. They have warranty offers of ten years and above. These panels are easy to mount, facing the rays of sunlight. You will find them in a wide range of sizes, and they are durable. If you want the best choice in performance and durability, consider purchasing and installing a rigid solar panel.

Portable Solar Panels

Consider buying portable solar panels if you want to mount a standalone or off-grid solar system. It is designed as a solar briefcase that could be stored in a vehicle. This will be pulled out and mounted on your camper. This is useful for charging phones, laptops, appliances, and other equipment outdoors.

Portable solar panels are more accessible, cheaper, and suitable for beginners. It is made to receive proper sunlight wherever you may park your vehicle. A portable solar panel is the best option if you live in a van.

This solar panel is designed for cars, RVs, vans, boats, and other vehicles. It enables you to harvest solar energy on the go. However, you need to mount it whenever you are camping.

Fixed Solar Panels

This type of solar panel is installed on top of the RV. You can adjust the angles manually using tilt mounts. This adjustment will enable you to harvest more sunlight. Photovoltaic panels are more efficient at moderate temperatures. Create a space between the top of your vehicle roof and the panel. It is not advisable to glue or screw panels directly to the rooftop. This makes the device lose air flowing at the base of the panel, which can cool the entire system.

Rigid panels are better than fixed panels as their frames are designed with space to permit airflow underneath the system.

Fixed panels constantly harvest sunlight whenever the sun is shining on your campsites. They could not be stolen easily and can take little space on the roof. They can provide up to 200 watts of solar power to your equipment and appliances.

In most cases, they serve as double shades on your vehicle rooftop for reducing heat in extreme weather conditions. These panels raise your roofline, making your vehicle more conspicuous in the camp. They are difficult to adjust the angles to receive more sunlight, especially during sun peak hours.

What to Consider Before Buying a Solar Panel

Some of the things to consider before buying a solar panel include:

Cost

Consider the cost of a solar panel before buying. Most times, cheap products don't last as long as we expect. They depreciate faster than high-quality ones. As much as you want to maintain your budget, remember that some cheaper panels may not deliver efficiently. They could be valuable for the short term. These inexpensive products may explode with intense heat from the atmosphere.

Warranty Offers

Solar panels come with warranties that define the longevity of the product. It is crucial to examine this feature before parting with your bucks. Most panels are designed to last for over twenty-five years. Therefore, ensure that your panel has a warranty that can cover those numbers of years.

Buying Used Solar Panels

If people want to save money on a car, they will often buy a slightly used one and have it checked out to learn about its history. The same can be said for houses and other items. When buying used items, all I can say is, "buyer, beware!"

Solar panels are most effective when purchased brand new. They will be at their most efficient and usually come with a warranty. Of course, many people cannot overcome the initial investment, regardless of how much money they may save in the long run. In this case, they may choose used solar panels to save money upfront. However, as with any other tool, there are potential pitfalls to be aware of. If you decide to go this route and look for used solar panels, keep the following things in mind.

Reduced Energy Output

The older solar panels become, the less power they can produce. This is particularly true if the panels are made of amorphous silicon. While this should not deter you from purchasing used solar panels, be aware that you may require more of them to match the efficacy of new ones. For example, ten used panels may be needed to equal the benefits of eight new ones. Again, this is dependent on the age of the solar panels. If you intend to buy extra old equipment to match the value of new equipment, it may be better just to buy new. Calculate the savings to find out where they are.

Tight Connections

When purchasing used panels, you may miss loose connections between the solar cells if you do not look closely enough. These sloppy connections can significantly reduce sunlight absorption. You can fix this problem by tightening the connections with the proper tools, but make sure the savings are worth the extra effort.

Panels that are Damaged

Solar panels can sustain significant damage over time. If you notice cracks in the glass, moisture beneath the cover, or completely broken connections, decide whether you want to fix the problems. If this is the case, the deal may still be worthwhile.

Unstable Current

Always test your panels for their efficacy. Used solar panels can often be damaged under the surface, where it's difficult to detect. Often, moisture can get into the internal circuitry, which can cause fluctuations in the voltage output. If you notice damaged seals, assume there is also some internal damage. Bad circuitry implies that the solar panels will not work.

Many people sell their solar panels because they want to upgrade to new ones. If you are ready to do the proper assessments, then sites like eBay are the best places to buy used solar panels. Always inspect the panels thoroughly and never let anyone rush you into doing so. If they do, this should be a huge red flag.

Solar Racking

Solar panels are not directly attached to your roof. They are mounted on a proper racking system, which also allows for creating a right angle to get optimal sun exposure. Good solar racks are essential to ensure your expensive panels are correctly installed. Not having proper racks is like having an expensive car with bad wheels. These rackings are usually made from aluminum, which works well for rooftop installations. Aluminum is strong, durable, and does not weigh much.

The Right Wire Type

Aluminum or Copper

You can use either copper or aluminum wire. Copper wire is slightly more expensive but suffers from fewer power losses. It is more flexible than aluminum and prevents overheating better.

Stranded or Solid

Solid wires have a single metal wire core, whereas stranded wires have multiple stranded wire cores.

Stranded wires typically have a larger diameter, greater flexibility, and superior conductivity, but they are more expensive.

Stranded wires are recommended (at least for outdoor cables) but are not required for your PV system.

When it comes to wiring, insulation is another critical factor. Your wires will be subjected to weather conditions, particularly if you are constructing a PV system for boats and RVs. As a result, you should think about UV, water, chemical, and heat resistance.

Wire names indicate what they are built for. Looking at those acronyms like that could be a little disorienting, but when you know their actual meaning, they will help you out.

- H stands for Heat resistant. Sometimes found as HH or High Heat.
- W stands for Water-resistant.
- R stands for Rubber insulation.
- T stands for Thermoplastic insulation.
- X stands for XLPE, which is Cross-Linked Polyethylene.
- N stands for Nylon insulation.

Now here are the different wires we can choose from:

- THHN is ideal for dry conditions. Withstands 194°F (90°C), not water.
- THWN / THWN-2 is suitable for conduit applications.
- RHW / RHW-2 is suitable for outdoor applications.
- XHHW / XHHW-2 have better resistance to chemical exposure and abrasion.
- USE-2 (Underground Service Entrance), ideal for underground wet conditions, can withstand higher pressure.

And then there is:

- PV Wire is designed explicitly for wiring Solar Panels since they can withstand water, extreme UV and heat exposure, and an extra layer of insulation.

Despite the color difference, all wires are equal (if they are the same type). But we use a specific color code to make maintenance more comfortable and safer.

DC Power

- Red: Positive Current wire
- Black: Negative Current wire
- Green: Earth (sometimes green with yellow stripes)
- White/Grey: Ground
- AC Power (120/208/240 Volts)
- Black: Phase 1
- Red: Phase 2
- Blue: Phase 3
- White: Neutral
- Green: Ground/Earth (sometimes green with yellow stripes)

Choosing the appropriate size of wires and cables is critical in every PV system. The right wire reduces energy loss and prevents overheating. And in fact, using undersized lines violates the National Electric Code (NEC) and will most probably bring you troubles

Thickness and Rating

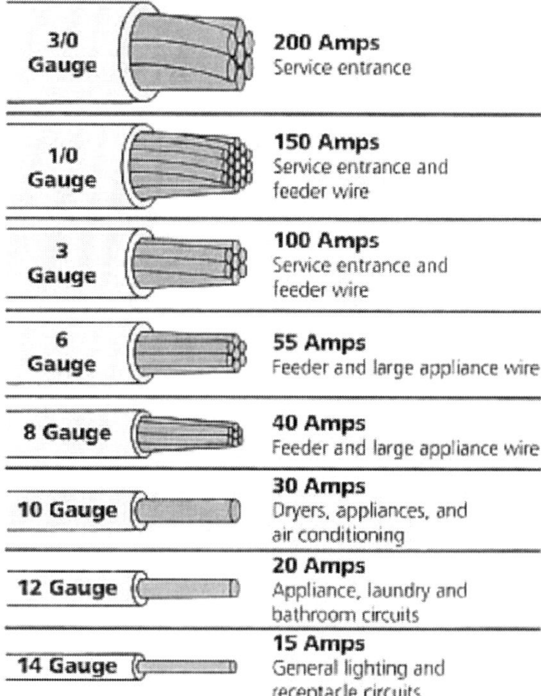

First, we will discuss the thickness closely related to a wire's rating.

The rating is what you will want to check since it determines how many currents the wire can handle safely. The US specifies it on the American Wire Gauge (AWG).

The AWG indicates (on its scale) the resistance of the wire. The lower the AWG, the less the resistance. And as you now know, the lower the resistance, the higher the current (Amps) it can deliver.

To deliver more and more Amps, a wire needs to have more and more metal wire cores. That's why a lower AWG rating means a thicker wire.

Length and Voltage Drop

You would think a wire is a wire, no matter how long, but this is not the case.

In fact, the longer the wire, the less the efficiency. The longer the distance electricity travels, the higher current is expended, and the more voltage drops.

With some calculations, we can keep that Voltage drop under 2-3%.

The Right Wire for the Right Use

Solar Panels to Combiner Box

Since it will be an outdoor application, the best choice is a PV Wire, but USE-2 and RHW-2 are valid alternatives.

As a general rule-of-thumb, each PV module can be paired with a 10-12 AWG wire.

When you buy Solar Panels, though, they often come with their cables, which are usually designed for this specific use—no need to look for other wires.

Combiner Box to Charge Controller

Here you can stop worrying about water. Your wires will likely run in dry conditions from the Combiner Box on. Therefore, THHN-2 will suffice.

Of course, if you are building a PV system for your boat, water will always be a security issue, so you may want to consider THWN-2 as well.

Here you will be looking for thicker wires with a lower AWG rating (3-8) since they will need to carry the Current from multiple Solar Panels.

Circuit Breakers and Isolator Switches

While fuses sacrifice themselves to save the day, Circuit Breakers can automatically disconnect the circuit in case of surges and have a much longer lifespan. That's a panel with a series of switches, usually connected to DC loads. Every home is equipped with one, so you should be familiar with it.

Isolator Switches, on the other hand, are just, well, switches that you can manually operate to break a circuit. They are usually used to isolate components and allow maintenance.

Chapter 4: Off-Grid System Design

DIY: Solar Power for Tiny Homes and Cabins

Many homeowners will live off-grid in remote homes located on the city's outskirts to reduce their reliance on worldly possessions and free themselves from dependence on the state for power. These smaller remote homes could be miniature versions of traditional houses or cabins. Even though they are small, these remote homes require electricity for lighting, heating, bathing, and cooking.

Important Questions to Ask Before Building

How Much Electricity Do You Intend to Produce?

Tiny homes typically use significantly less electricity than larger homes. However, the amount of load on each tiny house will vary based on how each family chooses to live, the equipment utilized, and the number of occupants. To save money, you should generate as much electricity as possible. This means you should have as many solar panels as you can afford.

Are You Putting in a Roof-Mounted or Ground-Mounted System?

Before anything else, decide where the system will be placed. If you plan to install solar panels on your roof, you must first determine whether the roof receives enough sunlight. Additionally, you can put your solar panels on the ground if the roof is sturdy enough to withstand and handle the weight of the panels without losing its integrity. These ground-mounted systems will necessitate additional racks and mounting hardware. Finally, ensure your panels are slightly tilted to capture as much sunlight as possible.

How Many Batteries are You Going to Need?

You will need a certain number of batteries to store excess solar power if you use an off-grid solar power system. The cells will be an essential component of the system because they will provide ample power during the night or when the weather conditions are unfavorable for powering solar panels. If you buy batteries, remember that they are sensitive to extreme weather fluctuations and can wear and degrade quickly when subjected to frequent temperature changes between freezing and hot. Many vendors offer whole solar kits that you may install in your home along with batteries (this will remove the hassle of deciding on the number of cells you have to buy).

Calculations for Your Off-Grid Tiny Home or Cabin

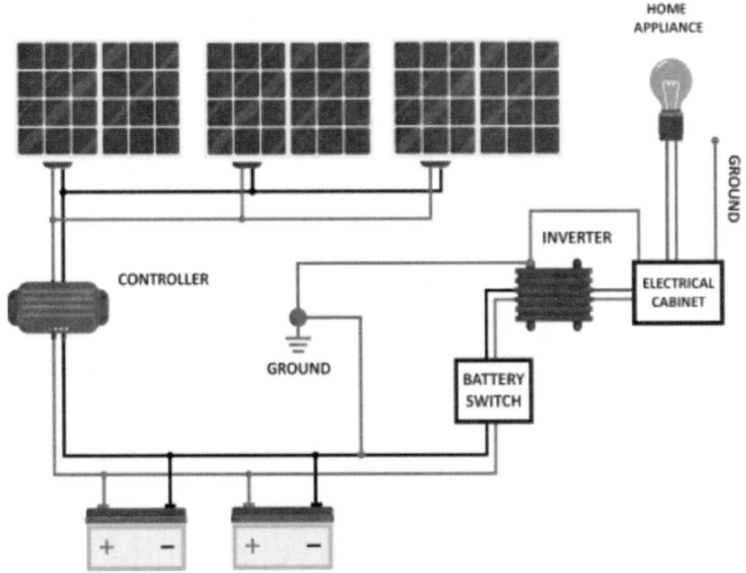

A cabin with only a propane heater, stove, a few lights, and a ceiling fan will consume less electricity than one with a running fridge, washing machine, electric stove, and other power-hungry gadgets. In essence, the first calculation you'll need to conduct to estimate the size of your solar power system is to calculate your house load. Let's make a few calculations and choose how many panels an average tiny home would require:

- Daily time spent under direct sunlight: 5 hours
- The average daily energy consumption: 100kWh per month
- The wattage of each solar panel: 290W

Using the data above, the typical solar power panel will generate 290W, which when multiplied by the quantity of hours in which it receives direct sunshine, results an amount just under 1,500kWh or 45kWh per month. This means that one solar panel has a capacity of 45kWh per month. You will need to add a few more panels in order to reach the monthly cap of 100kWh:

- 1 standard solar panel = 45KWh

- 2 standard solar panels = 90kWh
- 3 standard solar panels = 135kWh
- 4 standard solar panels = 180kWh

Therefore, a tiny home would need around 2 to 3 solar panels to meet power needs. However, you must get four regular solar panels for this type of residence in order to leave additional room in the system for unforeseen power usage.

How to Mount Solar Panels on Vehicles and Tiny Homes

Before mounting solar panels on your vehicles, you must evaluate your need for energy on the campground. How much equipment need to use electrical current in the camp. These considerations will help you to decide how many solar panels to mount on your cars, RVs, vans, and boats.

Again, you should decide the size of the inverter you need for the setup, battery, and solar system sizes. Also, check the charge controller size. This assessment will help you to know if the solar system requirements are too expensive or large for your campers or vehicles.

Wiring the panels could be done in series or parallel. Series wiring involves connecting the positive axis of one panel to the negative axis of another in the series. This helps to increase the voltage. However, amperage remains the same.

In parallel wiring, all positive wires of the panels are connected to a single combiner and then plugged into the charge controller. All the negative wires of the panels are connected to another single combiner. In this case, the voltage remains the same, but the amperage increases in the charge controller.

DIY: Solar Power for RVs and Boats

Off-grid solar power systems for small boats and RVs have the same structural components but range in size (depending on the power requirements). For example, one home may only need a 5W panel to keep the solar batteries charged between a few road trips or sailing trips per year. Otherwise, homeowners living full-time in their small boat or RV may need 900W solar panels, a large battery bank, and an inverter. Generators are also common on most off-grid RV and sailboat solar systems.

Most RV and boat light bulbs and small accessories operate on 12 volts of direct current (DC); solar panels and batteries can easily power these lights. Switch to more energy-efficient electrical appliances to reduce the power required in a solar power system. Using DC fluorescents, for instance, can greatly minimize the amount of solar panels required in your system (an excellent product would be the Thin-Lite 12V fluorescent light bulb). These bulbs provide the same amount of light as a standard incandescent light bulb while using roughly one-third of the power that incandescent light bulbs do.

But because they are more expensive and of inferior quality than regular household appliances, I warn you against buying exclusively 12-volt appliances. I've also discovered that most RVs come with an inverter ranging from 250W for powering small electrical appliances to 4,000W pure sine wave, with a built-in battery charger.

Key Considerations Before Building in Your RV or Boat

Depending on how much power is used, each RV or boat will require a different number of panels. For instance, anticipate to utilize 80W to 130W of panels and a deep-cycle solar battery to power the lights, a small TV, and other commonplace devices in a mobile home. However, you would often require 200W to 450W of solar panels if you need an inverter to power a microwave, vacuum, coffee maker, and other AC equipment.

Batteries

The battery requirements for each home will vary; however, modest RVs and campers will need at least a 200 to 225 amp-hour capacity. However, consider the space you have to store a battery bank, limiting the number of batteries you can purchase. For instance, you might require 800 amp-hours of capacity but only have space for 400 amp-hours; in this case, the amount of power you can utilize in your home would be limited. It is crucial to keep in mind that combining different types of batteries in one set or using old batteries with new cells when connecting your batteries could result in issues with your system.

You must determine how many watts you will need each day in order to calculate how much battery power (in amp-hours) you will need. For you to never run out of electricity, one might infer that your battery bank should be able to provide at least twice as much power as you need each day. If a 12-volt battery has a 100 AH capacity, for example, it can provide 1200 watts; nevertheless, you shouldn't try to use the whole 1200 watts because doing so would damage the battery. Instead, leave 50% power in each battery or use 600 watts at most.

Inverters

Some people prefer to utilize a compact inverter that is inexpensive and capable of powering light loads, such laptops and other electrical gadgets. However, others will require a large inverter that can run coffee machines or microwaves. These larger inverters can cost between $500 and $1,100 and supply 800 to 1200 watts of power. Most smaller RVs or houseboats use inverters that provide around 1000 watts to 1500 watts.

Mounting a Solar Array

For most boats and RVs, I would recommend a flat or tilted mounting system. There are many benefits of tilting mounts; one is they offer 10 to 20% more power production under normal weather conditions. For those who are constantly on the move, tilting your solar array on an RV rooftop can be a problem because it necessitates parking the RV so that it can face straight south and benefit from the sunlight. In addition, I advise against leaving the tilting mounts on the roof of a moving car because doing so could harm the foundation. In order to limit shifting while driving and always get the most of the sun, you should think about mounting your solar array flat on the RV roof.

Calculations for an Off-Grid RV or Boat

You cannot disregard the cost consequences of owning one of these systems while developing an off-grid solar power system for an RV or houseboat. Therefore, you will need to do some calculations to determine whether one of these systems will be feasible to own. Simple counts of a typical medium-power RV or boat system are provided here:

- 1 or 2 X 80 to 150-watt solar panels.
- 1 X panel mount, which you will install on the roof of your vehicle or boat.
- 1 X solar charge controller.
- 4 X 220 amp-hour 6-volt deep cycle batteries (a battery that can power a golf cart).
- 1 X 600 to 1,500-watt solar inverter.

This type of system's overall cost might range from $400 for smaller systems to $4,000 for bigger systems (with some of these large systems including a sine wave inverter). With the example used above, the total energy output per day would come to 1600 watt-hours. This would be enough power to effectively run the lighting system and the appliances in your mobile home with no issues.

Schematic for RV with an external power supply:

Racking

Racking is also known as mounting. It is one of the main components of a solar power system. The panel is appropriately secured onto the roof using the racking system. High-quality racking devices are used to attach the solar panels onto the roof. Mounting the panels should be done by reputable installation companies to avoid hazards.

Mobile Solar Panel Designs

Photovoltaic module designs for mobile applications should be able to quickly deploy and orient the modules in the sun while also being compact enough to be transported. They are made of aluminum profiles with stainless steel fasteners and rotary nodes that allow you to change the geometry and orientation of the entire system or individual elements. Such designs are subject to certain constraints related to the overall system's weight and size and the conditions for transportation and bringing it up to working order.

As previously stated, the performance of photovoltaic systems directly depends on how correctly solar panels are installed and the designs for the chosen. A photovoltaic system's selection and design calculation are as crucial as the system's other components - photovoltaic modules and inverters - in obtaining maximum energy output.

Active use of renewable energy sources contributes to the growing use of solar cells in building cladding. Photovoltaic modules (PV), when integrated into the building envelope, take on new functions that are not limited to electricity generation. Simultaneously, the requirements for these systems are increasing and becoming more stringent.

Photovoltaic modules are available with flat or flexible surfaces and cellular or multilayer structures. They can be embedded in any part of the building envelope and used as a design element due to their characteristics (size, flexibility, shape, and appearance). Photovoltaic modules are used with traditional architectural materials such as glass and metal in opaque and translucent forms.

Most photovoltaic modules are designed as auxiliary elements that only produce energy. The module sizes are optimized to collect energy and facilitate assembly, with little consideration for integration issues into the building's architecture and construction. As a result, their installation and operation raise numerous concerns. The main source of the problem is photocell manufacturers' insufficiently high competence, which is usually associated with a lack of appropriate standards.

Photovoltaic modules must be developed following specific technical requirements while also combining building envelope functions (so they can be easily mounted on the roof, facade, parapet, etc.), reliable and safe. The built-in module must meet more stringent criteria than the traditional one (in terms of thermal and mechanical resistance). This is critical, especially in today's environment, where there are no standards governing this issue.

Photovoltaic modules and installations are self-contained devices that convert solar energy into electrical energy. As a result, traditional photovoltaic systems are only thought of as photovoltaic energy generators. A pressing issue in the field of photovoltaic systems is that, on the one hand, the market requires cost-effective solutions based on photovoltaic systems (module cost per watt peak load). On the other hand, manufacturers must develop new equipment independently, incurring high costs. In theory, photovoltaic systems can be installed on any part of the building envelope that receives direct sunlight. They are typically installed on the roof, facades, and sun visors.

Photovoltaic systems are installed using three methods: adding photovoltaic modules, replacing a portion of the enclosing structures, and integrating the modules into the enclosing structures. The building envelope features, architecture, and energy characteristics should be noted when using them. When used on a glazed facade, for example, a module made of translucent double-sided glass should also serve as an insulating element with the required thermal insulation, insolation regulation, glare protection, and so on.

Photovoltaic panels have two main applications in a building: adding photovoltaic panels on top of the building envelope (building added photovoltaics, BAPV); and replacing parts of the building envelope with built-in photovoltaic panels (building-integrated photovoltaics, BIPV).

Traditional photovoltaic modules with appropriate mounting systems are typically used for elements mounted on top of the building envelope or BAPV. BAPV modules include various photovoltaic elements installed on the building's facade and many traditional photovoltaic systems for roof installation, typically after the building's completion. Photovoltaic modules usually do not have any special requirements because they serve no additional functions for the building. It is sufficient to run a series of IEC tests with minor adjustments.

Simultaneously, photovoltaic modules designed to replace traditional building envelope elements must compensate for all functions of the removed element. This means that the BIPV module, built into the building envelope, must meet more criteria than a standard photoelectric module. There are currently no standards governing this issue. As a result, the system must adhere to several standards, including electrical and building product standards. However, suppose the manufacturer of the photovoltaic module guarantees compliance with IEC standards and indicates this in its passport. In that case, construction requirements are still not included in the module certification and labeling procedure.

BOOK 3

Chapter 5: Mounting the Solar Panel on Your Roof

To mount your solar panel on your roof, you will first climb on the rooftop and sketch a rough plan of how the solar panel will be on the rooftop, considering everything present on the rooftop.

The first thing to do is to assess the condition of the roof to establish the remaining life span of the current roof. The entire roof surface must be inspected carefully to identify any points needing repair. In addition, any problems with moisture or seepage should be investigated and dealt with accordingly. It is essential to ensure a useful life of the roof of at least 20 years - the typical life of a photovoltaic system and government incentives - to avoid the cost of removing the photovoltaic system to carry out repairs on the roof. If the roof is made of Eternit or contains asbestos, installing the photovoltaic panels is an excellent opportunity to proceed with the roof renovation, given the potential danger that such a roof poses to human health. In addition, an expert must assess the roof's resistance to the weight of the panels and the strong winds that hit them.

Installation of PV Panels on Flat Roofs

Load the photovoltaic panels onto the roof first, carefully so as not to damage the roof covering. Then you choose an east-west direction for the linear metal supports (stainless steel, galvanized steel, or aluminum) to which the panels will be attached, which must be oriented south. Many structures are fixed by drilling holes in the roof and using dowels, but ballasts allow pre-assembled frames to be installed on a flat roof without drilling holes. Apply sealant around the holes in the first case to ensure a watertight seal and prevent moisture from entering the building. Finally, assemble the panels, which will be raised concerning the roof, and make the necessary electrical connections.

PV Panel Installation on Pitched Roofs

Photovoltaic panels can be attached to pitched roofs - that is, on pitched roofs (typically at an angle similar to the ideal angle to maximize solar radiation) - using special metal frames that are cut to size and allow partial or total integration with the roof itself. These supports provide a high level of safety against snow and wind loads and a high level of resistance to corrosion by atmospheric agents. The first step in assembly is to secure the anchorage brackets and relative uprights to the roof with expansion bolts or chemical inserts, after which the actual panel-holder frame will be mounted once the holes have been properly sealed. This allows you to create panel matrices with a single row or many adjacent rows. In the latter case, a suitable connection profile will connect each row of panels to the previous one. Finally, the system's electrical connections will be made.

Panels Integrated into Pitched Roofs are Installed

A photovoltaic system, in addition to being partially integrated on the roof as previously described, can replace the roof entirely or be "architecturally integrated," as the term goes. In this case, the first step is to install a double waterproofing sheath on the "bare" roof, which will then support the photovoltaic panels. As is customary, we begin by securing the metal brackets with expansion plugs, chemical inserts, or other adequate strength systems. To prevent infiltration through the anchor screws, these brackets are then covered with a layer of bituminous sheath. The uprights that will support the frame are then connected to the brackets. Stainless steel screws are typically used as screws because they resist deterioration over time. Still, special locking systems can be used to protect the customer from any attempts to steal the panels.

Structure Configuration for a Pitched Roof Photovoltaic (PV) Systems

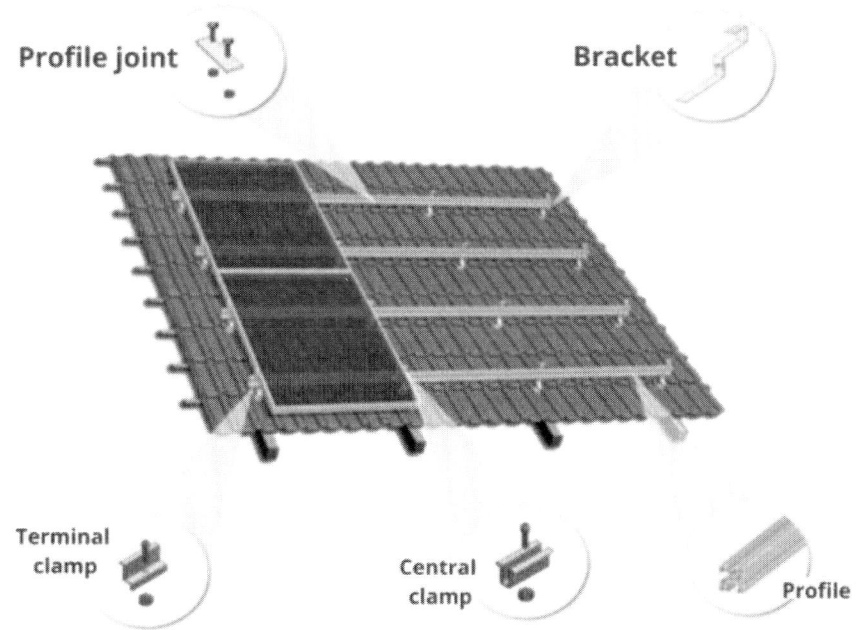

PV System Support Structure 1 kW x 4 Modules

This structure can be used to install a 1KW photovoltaic system on a pitched roof, consisting of four modules divided into two rows of two modules each:

8th bracket In wood or concrete roofs, we recommend using two brackets for each profile row.

- 32x32mm profile from 2,15 mt - 4 rows n° 4
- n° 4 central panels stop clamp
- n° 8 panels stop terminal clamp

8 Module Structure for 2kw Photovoltaic Systems

This structure can be used to install a 2KW photovoltaic system on a pitched roof consisting of 8 modules divided into two rows of 4 modules each:

12th bracket In wood or concrete roofs, we recommend three brackets for each profile row.

- Profile 32x32mm from 2,60 mt - 4 rows n° 4
- Profile 32x32mm from 1,60 mt - 4 rows n° 4
- Panel stop terminal clamp n° 8 Central panel stop clamp n° 12

8 Structure for 3kw Photovoltaic Systems - 12 Modules

This structure can be used to install a 3KW photovoltaic system on a pitched roof, consisting of 12 modules divided into two rows of 6 modules each:

- Bracket number 20. We recommend using five brackets, one every 1.30mt, for each profile row.
- Profile 32x32mm - 4 rows n° 8 Profile 32x32mm - 4 rows n° 4 Profile joint n° 8 Central panel stop clamp n° 20 Panel stop terminal clamp n° 8

Pole Mounting

Pole mount falls into two categories; single-pole and multi-pole structures.

Single Pole Mount

Single pole mounts include just a single upright pole used to support the solar panel mounted on the top of the pole or the pole's side. (If you are mounting your panel on the side of the pole, you can only mount an array within a range of one to four panels.

However, if you mount it on the top of the pole, you can mount an array ranging from ten to twelve panels).

Multi-Pole Mount

This mount usually carries about one or more vertical poles, with a horizontal pole joining the vertical supports.

Assembly Instructions

1. Determine the fixing point based on the design. Adjust the height of the brackets to fit your needs as you move the tiles.
2. Fix the profiles on the brackets
3. Join the profiles together with the joints.
4. Secure the ends of the first module to the profile with end clamps.
5. Attach the next module to the first one using the central clamps.
6. Place the final module on the profile and secure the ends with end clamps.

Chapter 6: The Process of Installing an Off-Grid Solar Power System

To begin, select the most energy-efficient PV panels for your home and region. Consider factors such as sunlight, roof area, and energy requirements. Remember that a more expensive model is more durable and practical because it captures more sunlight and resists wear and tear. Additional components such as the battery, charge controller, wiring, and inverter should also be high quality.

Solar panels are intended to produce clean, renewable energy. Choosing a suitable solar panel is the first step on your journey to green energy. If you cannot install the solar panels yourself, hire a professional installer.

It is time to begin installing your system if you are ready to dive and have all the necessary permits. Hopefully, you've purchased all of the essential equipment. While all of this material is quite durable, make sure to take all the required precautions. Even if you intend to hire a professional installer, understanding these steps will help you stay informed.

Location! It is critical to consider where you will physically place your panels. Once you've gathered your materials, conduct a thorough survey of your property to determine the best location for your panels. Remember, it's not just about which part of your roof gets the most sun. The pitch and direction of the roof also play a role. All these factors will determine which location will give your panels the most exposure for most of the day.

You must select a suitable platform after determining the location of your panels. These platforms can be flat or slightly inclined to face the sun. This should save you the trouble of building a custom platform if you have a good, solid roof. As I previously stated, ensure that your roof receives the necessary maintenance before beginning your installation process.

If your roof is insufficient for solar panels, you will need four concrete pillars and several pieces of 4x4 wood. The number of panels determines the amount of wood required. The conduit protects your wiring and other delicate materials that require a secure connection from the platform to your home. Again, a shorter conduit is usually required if your roof serves as your platform.

Many solar panels include mounting brackets that you can easily attach to your platform, mainly if it is wood. A good drill is required for steel platforms or roofs. If your panels did not come with brackets, ask the manufacturer if they can be provided or where you can get them. In addition, inquire about how to install the brackets on your solar panels.

Start securing the brackets' front feet when you're ready to mount. Before securing them with screws or other mounting material, ensure they are wholly squared and centered. It is time to attach the rear legs after obtaining meteorological data to determine the sun's movements in your area. By the way, I am aware that the Earth, not the sun, moves, but please bear with me for the sake of these instructions.

Once you've determined these dimensions, use the rear legs to elevate and tilt the solar panels in the best direction and angle. This will ensure that the panels receive the maximum amount of sunlight. Based on your calculations, make adjustments to your back legs. After that, secure the legs to the panel. You can make changes later, but it's best to get it right the first time.

This is possibly the most important part of the installation process, and I cannot emphasize how important it is to understand how the wiring works. This is true even if you do not do the wiring yourself, as you will be able to troubleshoot any performance issues or other issues.

A junction connector or a fuse combiner box will be required. You must connect the solar panels to the conduit. Before joining the panels to the fuse box mounted on the platform, the wires on the panels should be stripped and wired in pairs. The terminal box must be connected to the stripped wire. The red wires connect the positive terminal, and the black wires connect the negative terminal. Following connection, the wires are fed through the junction box's bottom and reconnected to the corresponding positive and negative terminal blocks.

A circuit breaker disconnect must be connected to the solar breaker. The energy will be transferred from the circuit disconnect to a charge controller and a battery bank. When necessary, energy is transferred from the batteries to the disconnect. It then flows from the disconnect to the power inverter, which converts the power from direct current to alternating current. The alternating current will then flow into your home's electric panel.

After you've figured out how the wiring for solar panels works, it's time to connect them to the house. To begin, route the electrical cable from the solar array into the house via the underground conduit. You can easily thread the cables through the conduit to the inverter panels if you connect them to a nylon rope. Connect these cables to the fuse combiner box located at the solar array's base. The green cables are connected to the grounding strip first, followed by the red cables to the positive terminal block and the black cables to the negative terminal block.

Solar system setups are more reliable and productive than other arrays due to various factors. These include:

Installation Guidelines

It is recommended that the homeowner purchases all the components mentioned above versus making them yourself. Be sure to follow the regional laws and install a risk-free system. The following instructions help determine the success or failure of a PV system installation:

A. Personnel

- Team effort is more suitable for full installations as they are complicated.
- A solar company, electrical sub-contractor, or electrician can be contacted.
- Company experts have more experience in PV systems compared to others.
- The team has to coordinate their services and install them per building codes.
- Solar power systems require inspections, meetings, and warranty assurance.

B. Standards of Safety

- Anything that has electricity and high voltages has to be safe.
- The installing team should protect the equipment, residents, and the property at all costs.
- The solar panels and circuits are categorized as electrical systems.
- The PV panel set-up has to satisfy electrical safety codes for your application area.
- During the installation, one should ensure the health and safety of all personnel.
- Eliminate the electrical hazards and risks associated with climbing high roofs.
- The installation experts should follow the best practices for their safety.

C. Wiring Rules

- Direct current (DC) wiring panel fixtures are usually very large-sized.

- The installing company should protect outdoor wiring against high temperatures, wind, and rain.
- One can drill the roofs for conduits, cabling, and electrical wiring.
- Make sure the roofs are sealed off with the help of construction experts.

D. System Design

- One can install a pre-engineered panel system based on their needs
- Carefully size the various parts for setting up a perfect PV system.
- The building's shade, roof angle, gable, etc., must be considered.
- Design the off-grid and grid-connected systems with precision.
- Solar companies, traders, and distributors can also plan and implement.

E. Costs

- One can use software tools for design and cost estimation.
- One can calculate the installation costs in "per watt" terms of energy.
- Efficiency and cost are inversely related to each other in PV panels.
- Labor charges depend on the complexity of the task (e.g., roof type and building layout).
- If the solar power system uses all the components, the cost increases.

Figure Out How Much Power You Need

Okay, plan a trip to Kazakhstan without determining how many miles it will take you to get there and, consequently, how much gas you will need. It seems a little rash, doesn't it? You can't just declare that you'll invest money in four solar-powered boards and two batteries and assume that's all you need. Remember that your structure serves as the fuel for everything. Determine the precise amount of effort needed. You can refer to this book or other resources for guidance on choosing your home force's requirements.

Calculate the Number of Batteries That You Need

When you know how much force you need, it is important to sort out the number of batteries needed to store this force.

- Do you have to only store power for two days, or would you like to have enough power stored for four days or more?
- Do you have a backup energy source, such as a turbine or generator, that can help you out when the sun isn't shining?
- Will your batteries be stored in a warmed room or a virus room?

The larger your battery bank should be, the colder the extra battery space. If your residence has temperatures below the point of solidification, you will require three batteries for every two that your companion in a radiant area employs.

- **Solar panel mounting location** – Shades or shadows should not be used to conceal it. Except for parallel panels, shading any panel affects the functionality of all other panels interconnected in that array.
- **The electrical system** – This could be either parallel or series wiring. If the panels are wired in series, any disruption in the line, such as damage to any part of the cable, could affect the overall system's functionality. However, in parallel wiring, each panel is wired differently, giving them autonomy. As a result, any line failure will only affect one or two of the panels in that array.

Solar Panel Structures and Features for Vehicles and Homes

Solar panels can have different structures and features. Flexible solar panels, rigid solar panels, portable solar panels, and fixed solar panels are examples of these.

Select a Solar Charge Controller and Inverter

The solar-powered charge controller and inverter have both been discussed in this book. It's crucial to have both if you want your framework to be as effective and perfect as is conceivably possible. This book and other resources can be used to help you choose the best items to purchase.

Consider the System Balance

This last advance is more similar to a few previous advances that you have to take:

- Do you have an ideal circuit and breaker box? There is no space for betting with an off framework. This book has just covered the wire and wire box issue.
- How are you going to mount your boards?
- Will you have them on a housetop or the ground?
- Will you do it without anyone's help, or will you have another person do it for you?

Determining the Number of Solar Panels Needed

The seasons in your area must be considered. It's important to know how much sun there is available for harvesting and how much power you require. Use the most direct approach imaginable in your region, so you never have to be concerned about losing power. You can use online resources to figure out how many solar boards you need.

To determine how many solar panels you will need for your home, you must first figure out some information beforehand. Mainly, you will need to understand your goals regarding investment, lowering your carbon footprint, and saving money in the long run. Remember that the more you rely on solar, the larger your initial investment will be, but the more savings you will have in the long run. You must consider the following criteria to calculate how many solar panels your home will need.

How Much Solar Power Will You Use?

You must determine your home's average energy requirements to determine your solar power needs. Look at your past utility bills to find this information. From here, multiply your hourly energy requirement by the peak sunlight hours in your area, then divide this number by the specific panel's wattage. Roof size and battery storage also play a role here.

Solar Panels fitting on a rooftop with plenty of surface area

How Many Watts of Energy Do You Currently Use?

On your energy bill, you will see a section that says, "Kilowatt-hours used," or some similar phrase. Also, note the period, which is generally 30 days, especially for a monthly bill. Finally, look at your daily average. If your bill does not have a daily average, divide your monthly average by 30 or yearly average by 365. To determine the hourly average, if not listed, divide the daily average by 24 to get your final answer. If you have an hourly average but no daily average, multiply the hourly by 24.

Whatever your daily energy usage is in kilowatts is what your target daily target for solar energy should be. This will cover most of your energy needs. Experts recommend adding an extra 25% cushion to your target daily average since solar panels do not work at maximum capacity due to weather and other factors. So, if your daily average is 30 kilowatts, 25% of this is 7.5, so account for 37.5 kilowatts daily needs.

How Much Sunlight Can You Expect?

The Peak sunlight hours for your specific location will impact the energy you can expect your solar power system to create. An area with fewer peak sunlight hours would require more panels to obtain the same results. For example, a home in Seattle would require more panels than a home in Phoenix or Maui.

Returning to question one, multiply your hourly usage by 1,000 to calculate watts. Divide the hourly average of wattage by the number of peak sunlight hours in your area. This final number will give you the amount of energy your panels, when combined, need to produce every hour, on average.

Solar panels with a layer of protective plastic are considered flexible solar panels. They are designed as fat cells and don't have a frame. These low-profile panels are bendable and can be fitted onto the rooftops of your vehicles, campers, and tiny houses.

Flexible solar panels are designed with soft plastic materials. They could be scratched easily and are lightweight. They are durable and may not damage easily if they impact them.

However, it is not advisable to bend the panels too much. This may cause disruptions in solar cells and affect internal connections. Due to issues of bendability and connectivity, the panel has a shorter period of warranty offers.

Flexible panels are not free-standing. They have limited exposure to the rays of sunlight. They are bendable up to thirty degrees and customizable to the structures of the surfaces they are being mounted.

This is suitable for the rooftops of vans, RVs, cars, and boats, especially if you don't want to borehole on the vehicles. This quality makes the whole panel easily exposed to constant sunlight. However, the panels become less efficient the more you bend them, as most parts may not be exposed to sunlight.

What Affects Solar Panel Efficiency?

The efficiency of a solar panel refers to how well it can convert sunlight into usable energy. Not all solar panels are alike, and photovoltaic panels, the most commonly used type for residential areas, can range from 150 to 370 watts per panel. Cell technology also plays a role here, as solar cells with no grid lines on the front absorb more sunlight than conventional cells. In addition, a microinverter on each panel can optimize power conversion over a single mounted inverter on the side of the house.

The key takeaway is that the more efficient the panels, the more wattage they can produce. In turn, the fewer panels you will need. This is where quality over quantity plays a role. If you are trying to get cheaper panels to save money, realize that you might need to buy more of them to gain the same energy outcomes.

To determine the number of solar panels you need, divide your home's hourly wattage that you calculated earlier by the wattage of the solar panels.

Does Solar Panel Size Play a Role?

The size of a solar panel can undoubtedly make a difference. However, a bigger panel does not mean it is better. The more important number to look at is the power rating. A comparable example would be batteries. A 9-volt battery is smaller than a D battery but produces more power. The same can be true for solar panels. Also, as technology has advanced, solar panels have become more efficient and smaller in physical size.

If you have a larger usable roof area, buying larger panels at a lower cost and reduced efficiency might be the way to go. Smaller, more expensive, and higher efficiency panels might be the way to go if you have a limited roof area. In short, size does make a difference, but not how you think.

After you answer the above questions, you will better understand how many solar panels are ideal for your situation. There is no one-size-fits-all answer here.

What's With the South?

I have mentioned facing the south a few times in this book. This is the optimal direction your solar panels should be facing for maximum efficacy of the system. We have been told countless times that the sun rises in the east and sets in the west. This fact has become common knowledge; however, it is not entirely accurate, which I will explain in my first point. The bottom line is that you want the most out of your solar power system, so you cannot just buy any old panel and plop it wherever you choose. You will be wasting both money and the efficiency of the product. I will go over some major reasons why the panels you install should be facing towards the south. There is a lot more to it than just leaving the panels in the sun.

Why is Direction Important?

The idea of the sun rising in the direction of the east and set in the west is only 100% if you live directly on the equator. Otherwise, it has a Southern offset, especially in the winter. The sun also does not travel in a straight line as the day progresses. It arches a little bit as it moves. To get a good visual of this, watch some time-lapse videos online.

This is why solar panels need to face southwards.

What About the Angles?

On top of the direction, the solar panels' angle also matters. There is some math involved when installing the panels. The proper angle is determined by the geographical latitude of the given location. This will produce the most amount of energy in a given year. Direction is Important

Assembling the Pieces

Buy the Cells

There are a couple of various solar cells to purchase, and most great options are either made in the United States, China, or Japan. Nonetheless, the best expense-to-proficiency choice is probably polycrystalline cells. The quantity of cells you should purchase depends upon the measure of energy you're hoping to obtain. The specs ought to be recorded when you buy the cells.

Make sure to purchase additional items. These cells are incredibly delicate. Cells can be effectively purchased online through sites like eBay; however, you may buy some from your nearby home improvement shop.

It might be important to clear wax off the cells if the producer ships them in wax. To do this, dunk them in hot, though not boiling, water.

Each cell shouldn't cost more than $1.30 per watt.

Measure and Cut a Sponsorship Board

You will require a dainty board made from a non-conductive material, such as glass, plastic, or wood, to append the cells. Determine the solar panel plan, and measure and slice a board to that size. Leave an additional inch or two on the ends for the wires that interface the lines. Wood is a basic sponsorship material to pick since it's simpler to penetrate, which you'll have to do for the cell wires to go through.

Measure and Cut the Entirety of your Selecting Wire

When you look at your polycrystalline cells, you'll see numerous little lines going one way and two bigger lines going the other way. You should associate a selecting wire with running down the two bigger lines and interfacing with the cell's back in the cluster. Measure the length of that bigger line, double the length, and cut two pieces for every cell.

Motion in the Work Territory

Using a motion pen, run two to three lines of transition down every cell strip's length or gather three squares. Make a point to do this on the back of the cells. This will shield the warmth of the patching from causing oxidation.

Bind the Selecting

Utilize a binding iron to place a slim layer of the patch onto the rear of the cell strips. This step is unnecessary if you buy pre-fastened selecting, which is regularly a superior choice since it cuts time, warms the cells a single time, and squanders less weld. Be that as it may, it's increasingly costly.

Bond the Wire to the Cells

Warm the main portion with a bit of selecting wire with a welding iron. Bond the wire's end to a cell. Rehash this holding procedure for every cell.

Protecting Your Equipment

If you bought a car, a piece of jewelry, or a new T.V., I imagine you would protect these items at all costs. The same should hold for your solar equipment. You will make a significant investment in these materials, and while they are built to last a while, you need to do your best to protect them and increase their longevity.

Remember that your solar panels will be exposed to the elements, and Mother Nature can sometimes be harsh. While you can't predict or control what happens in your environment, you can take precautions to keep your valuable equipment safe and secure. In this section, I'll go over a few of them.

Hail Protection for Solar Panels

Hail can cause significant damage to cars, homes, and other objects caught in its path. They can vary in size and can occasionally be larger than golf balls. Unfortunately, solar panels are not resistant to hailstorms. The good news is that most manufacturers understand the problems caused by hail and specifically design their panels to reduce the risk of damage as much as possible. Any reputable brand has put its products through rigorous testing. Of course, what happens in a controlled environment versus what happens outside in the elements can be very different.

While modern solar panels are nearly hail-proof, there are some extra precautions you can take to reduce damage further. If you invest thousands of dollars in a new system, you might as well take all the precautions you can, just like any other expensive item.

Add a Methylcrylate Layer

This is a type of additional armor or plate made of plastic that helps to shield the panels further and make them more durable. A thin layer should be applied as carefully as possible to the most vulnerable areas of a panel. Take care not to obstruct the power supply's access line.

The higher the quality of your plates, the more impact they can withstand. You may have to spend more money, but your solar panels will be better protected.

Instead of methyl acrylate, cut a piece of plexiglass one inch larger than the panel's dimensions. Assemble the plexiglass on top of each panel, leaving a small gap between each layer. This will provide plenty of protection.

Angles are Important Once More

Another viable option for hail protection is to mount your solar panels on a pole and tilt them vertically when a hail forecast is issued. Most hailstones will slide down the side of the panels rather than hitting them directly.

Weather Forecasts

Keeping up with the weather can keep you informed of any impending hail storms on the horizon. This is more than just watching the weather channel. You can also get weather apps for your phone or visit your local weather station to stay updated. A detailed report from the weather station will notify you of any serious weather attacks in the forecast.

Examining the weather report to be ready for any potential hail storms or conditions

Add Solar Panels to Your Policy

As soon as you get your solar panels and equipment, ensure your homeowners' insurance covers them. If they aren't, request that they be added. This type of insurance can cover a large portion of the damage to your solar power system. Also, keep your warranty information handy. Find out how long it lasts and what is included.

Most solar panels today can withstand hailstones up to one inch in size and winds up to 50 miles per hour. As a result, they can withstand a great deal of force. Most hail storms will have little impact, but it's still a good idea to take as many precautions as possible.

Falling Debris Damage

A lot of debris falls from the sky, and a lot ends up on our roofs. You'll understand precisely what I mean if you've cleaned out a gutter. Debris can be as small as leaves and small twigs or as large and more damaging materials as rocks and tree branches. While solar panels are extremely durable, they can still be damaged by flying garbage. This is especially true when we go without checking on our system for long periods.

On the other hand, smaller debris causes micro-scratches on the solar panels. These scratches may not appear significant, but they can significantly reduce solar energy absorption because sunlight will not shine directly on the solar cells. As a result, your home's energy output will be reduced. Larger debris can destroy panels.

While it is impossible to eliminate all debris, a few extra precautions can be taken to mitigate its effects. The most obvious solution is to ensure that no trees or other structures are directly over the solar panels from which objects could fall. If this is not an option, at the very least, keep your trees maintained by pruning them. You won't have to choose between your trees and solar panels, and trees provide numerous benefits.

Additionally, do not allow debris to accumulate on your roof. This will reduce the efficiency of your panels and the energy output to your home significantly. Cleaning up smaller debris with a microfiber cloth and a garden hose will keep your solar power system clean. Doing this once a season is sufficient, but you can choose to do it more frequently. If you live in an area where debris is constantly flying around, monthly cleanings, at the very least, may be ideal. Simply put, if your solar panels appear dirty, clean them.

Water Stains on the Panels

Old and deteriorated seals typically cause water damage to solar panels. This is similar to windowpane insulation or sealing. This sealant around the solar panels becomes less effective as it ages, allowing water to leak. This can eventually lead to the components in the solar panels short-circuiting. Take the time to reseal your panels regularly to avoid seal damage.

Protection from Thieves

Because solar panels are costly, they invite robbers and thieves to come and steal them while they are unguarded. When installing your solar power system, it is critical to take precautions against theft. The following are some methods for safeguarding your solar panels.

- Install an alarm system. In a matter of minutes, thieves can dismantle your solar panels. So, you could go to bed one night or leave for work one morning, only to discover that some of your panels are missing the next time you look at them. You can add an alarm system to your panels that will sound if there is any movement. You will be notified via your smartphone or your alarm provider.
- Install motion detector lights near your panels on your roof to alert you to any suspicious activity.
- Keep track of the serial numbers on each panel. In the event of theft, authorities can use these numbers to locate your panels.
- Connect the solar panels. Because items are much stronger in groups, linking panels together makes it difficult to remove one easily and difficult to take a whole bunch without getting caught. A thief will usually give up and flee quickly.
- Once you start buying solar equipment, you will understand the value and want to protect it as much as possible. If you are willing to invest, take whatever precautions to keep it working for years to come.

Associating The Cells

Paste the Cells into the Board

Put a limited quantity of paste at the back focal point of the cells and press them into place. The selecting wire should run in a solitary, straight line. Ensure the selecting wire closes are coming up between the cells and are allowed to move, with simply the two pieces standing up between every cell. Ensure that one column runs toward the path inverse to the one close to it so that the selecting wire stands out toward the finish of one line and on the contrary side of the following. You should plan to place the cells in long lines with fewer lines. For instance, three columns, each comprising 12 cells, put long side to long side. Remember to leave an additional inch (2.5 cm) at the two closures of the load up.

Patch the Cells Together

Apply a transition to the length of the two thick lines (contact cushions) on every cell. Take the free areas of selecting wire and bind them to the cushions' whole length. The selecting wire associated with the rear of one cell should interface with the following cell's front for each situation.

Toward the start of the primary line, weld the selecting wire to the front of the main cell. The selecting wire should be about an inch (2.5 cm) longer than expected to cover the lines and reach out towards the board's additional hole. Patch those two wires along with a transport wire piece similar to the separation between the thick lines of the cell.

Associate the Subsequent Column

Interface the finish of the main column to the start of the second with a long transport wire piece that stretches out between the wire at the edge of the board and the wire that is the furthest away in the following line. You should set up the primary cell of the second column with an extra selecting wire, as you did with the first. Connect each of the four wires to this transport wire.

Keep Interfacing the Remainder of the Columns

Keep interfacing the columns with the long transport wires until you arrive at the end, associating it with a short transport wire once more.

Building Your Panel Box

Take your Cell Board Measurements

Calculate the space occupied by the board on which you have placed your cells. You will require a large container. Allow 1 inch (2.5 cm) on each side to accommodate the case. Leave space for this if there won't be a free 1-inch by 1-inch (2.5 cm x 2.5 cm) square spot at each corner after including the board. Try to leave enough room at the end for the transport wires.

Reduce the Level

In addition to the space for the crate sides, cut a piece of pressed wood to match what you estimated in advance. Depending on what you have available, you can use a table saw or a jigsaw.

Create the Sides

On the long sides of the case's base, measure two 1-inch by 2-inch (2.5 cm x 5 cm) bits of non-conductive board. Then cut two 1-inch by 2-inch (2.5 cm x 5 cm) boards to fit between these long pieces, completing the case. Cut the estimated pieces and secure them together with deck screws and butt joints. The sides should not be too tall because they may obscure the cells when the sun shines from a sharp point.

Attach the Sides

Screw through the head of the sides and into the base with deck screws to secure the gatherings to the case's base. The length of the sides determines the number of screws you use per side; however, regardless of length, you should not use fewer than three.

The Crate Should Be Painted

You can paint the crate any color you want. Consider using white or other light colors as this will keep the container cooler; cool cells perform better. If you use paint designed for outdoor use, your board will last longer. This type of paint will help protect the wood from the elements.

Add the Solar Panel to the Case

Paste the solar unit into the finished box. Ensure that it is secure and that the cells are looking up to take in daylight. Two openings should be on the board to finish the transport wire.

Wiring Your Panel

Associate the Last Transport Wire to a Diode

Get a diode somewhat greater than your board's amperage and associate it to the transport wire, protecting it with some silicone. The light-shaded end of the diode ought to point towards where the negative end of the battery goes. The opposite end ought to be wired to the negative finish of your board. This keeps energy from going back through the solar board from the battery when it isn't charging.

Associate Different Wires

Associate a dark wire to the diode and run it to a terminal square, which you should mount on the crate's side. Then associate a white wire from the short transport wire on the contrary side to the terminal square.

Interface your Board to a Charge Controller

Buy a charge controller and interface the board to the controller to associate the positive and negative effects. Run the wires from the terminal square to the charge controller, utilizing shading coded wire to monitor the charges. If using more than one board, you should associate the entirety of the positive and negative wires using rings to ensure you end up with two wires. Associate the charge controller to your batteries. Purchase batteries that will work with the size of the boards you assembled. Interface the charge controller to the batteries as indicated by the maker's directions.

Utilize the Batteries

When you have the batteries associated and charged from the board or boards, you can run your hardware off the batteries, depending on the intensity you need.

Fixing The Box

Get a Bit of Plexiglass

Buy a bit of plexiglass sliced to fit inside the container you made for your board. You can get this from a forte shop or your nearby home improvement shop. Make sure you get plexiglass, not glass, as glass is liable to break or chip.

Connect Square Stops for the Glass

Cut 1 inch by 1 inch (2.5 cm x 2.5 cm) squares of wood to fit into the corners. This ought to be sufficiently high to fit over the terminal square yet low enough to fit underneath the case's lip. Paste these stops into place utilizing a wood stick.

Supplement your Plexiglass

Fit the plexiglass onto the crate with the goal of the glass laying on the squares' heads. Using suitable screws and a drill, cautiously screw the plexiglass into the squares.

Seal the Case

Utilize a silicone sealant to seal the edges of the case. Additionally, seal any holes you can discover so that the container is as watertight as possible. Utilize the maker's guidelines to apply the sealant appropriately.

Mounting Your Panels

Mount Your Boards on a Truck

One option is to manufacture and mount your boards on a truck. This fix put the board at a point yet still permits you to alter which course the board countenances to adjust the amount of sun it gets in a day. Expect to change the board two to three times each day.

Install Your Boards on Your Roof

This is a popular method of mounting the boards because it results in the solar panels receiving the most sunlight and remaining off the beaten path. Regardless, the edge should be consistent with the sun's path and your peak load time. This limits you to only receiving full presentations at specific times. This option is ideal if you have a lot of boards and not much ground space to put them on.

Attach Your Boards to a Satellite Stand

The stands commonly used to mount satellite dishes can also be used to mount solar panels. They can even be made to move in tandem with the sun. However, this option will work best if you only have a few solar boards.

Are Solar Panels Harmful?

Despite the massive amount of data circulating about solar panels being harmful, modern crystalline silicon solar panels contain no poisonous materials. The 'poisonous solar panels' cases stemmed from the widely obsolete flimsy film (cadmium telluride - CdTe) solar panels, which contained cadmium and telluride levels. Nonetheless, unless these (rare) panels are separated into pieces, the following amount of cadmium is contained within the EVA layers and cannot be removed.

Current crystalline silicon solar panels have a trace amount of lead in the weld used for cell interconnections. In any case, the use of bind is gradually being phased out in favor of new busbar pressure joining methods and conductive glue materials. Its significant bind is used in numerous electrical devices and apparatuses. There are unquestionably, increasingly hazardous components used in consumer electronic devices, cell phones, computers, and televisions, which is why electronic waste, or e-waste, is a major global issue.

Ninety-eight percent of solar panels introduced today are of the crystalline silicon variety and do not contain cadmium or telluride. Solar panels are gentle, and when damaged, the cells do not contaminate the environment because they are epitomized and have no immediately solvent materials. Solar panels, like other devices, should be collected and reused until the end of their useful life, which we will discuss below.

Using Old Solar Panels

Because most solar panels introduced in the last 20 years have been used, there is not much solar waste. Many frameworks may reach the end of their useful life (EOF) over the next 10-20 years, resulting in an increase in the volume of solar-related waste that must be reused. Because of the easily reused materials, such as aluminum casings and mounting frameworks, solar panel reusing is a growing industry. Most solar panel manufacturers are striving to be more environmentally friendly. They are now a member of the non-profit PV Cycle association, which states that "PV CYCLE offers individuals and waste holders better access to reclaim and guarantees reusing rates over business principles."

In Europe, the French waste administration organization Veolia has opened the leading solar panel reusing office in southern France, which can recuperate and reuse 95% of the materials.

Connecting Every Part of the Solar System Together

Before connecting your system, ensure that all the disconnect switches are ***turned off***. You should follow a specific process to hook up all the units carefully.

The last component to connect to your solar system is the solar panels. Before connecting the solar panels to a charge controller, connect them to the battery bank. Connecting your PV panels to a charge controller before other components can be dangerous. It could cause a fire in the system or a massive explosion.

The system will turn on after you install the batteries and connect them to the charge controller unit; some settings will work in that mode.

Each solar panel comes with installation instructions. Complete the setup processes by following the instructions. Connect the inverter to the batteries after that. The solar panels are the final component of your solar setup.

If you do not want to go through this customizable process of installing your solar array, you can buy Ready Made Solar Systems. Goal Zero Solar System is one of the best brands, and this model is from them. This type is appropriate for off-grid use or living in a camp or other outdoor setting.

Ready-made solar systems are solar power generation units that are entirely self-contained. This is a ready-to-use integration of inverters, batteries, charge controllers, and other components. It is a simple device that allows you to connect directly to your solar panels or Goal Zero solar panels.

This solar system configuration is suitable for RVs, cars, vans, boats, and tiny houses. It will assist you in powering your appliances and living comfortably off the grid system. You can live in remote areas. With a functional, noiseless solar backup generator, you can live in the middle of a city or the middle of nowhere.

It is now time to connect the solar array to the grounding system. This ensures that the panels are safe to touch. To begin, bury a grounding rod about six inches of its body protruding above ground. This can be done on a wood surface or the ground directly. After that, connect a copper wire from the rod to the fuse box and another from the solar panels to the fuse box. This will safely ground the panels, allowing you to continue the installation.

Following the grounding procedure, the home connections must be established. Return to the building to finish the wiring. Connect the solar array to the inverter panel disconnect. Once again, red is connected to the positive terminal, green is connected to the grounding terminal, and black is connected to the negative terminal.

You can choose where to put the battery bank. However, it is recommended to be placed near the control panels. Run the conduit through the ceiling into the inverter panel from here. Two heavy-duty battery cables should be fed into the panel disconnect. The cable's opposite ends will be connected to the battery pack. The battery system must be connected and properly secured, alternating between positive and negative. After finishing this step, cover the panels to protect them. You now have a working solar power system. From here, you simply need to run some tests on the system to ensure it is working correctly. Turn on the power and check how the system works.

I admit that the installation procedure is complicated. At times, it can be physically demanding and intricate. Take your time and be very careful to avoid making any mistakes. The last thing you want is to invest significantly in your panels only to have them installed incorrectly. If you're not feeling at ease, don't be afraid to hire a professional. In the long run, the investment will be worthwhile. A professional will also ensure that all regulatory aspects of a solar power system are met. The basics of solar energy: The sun, the panel, the receiver

BOOK 4

Chapter 7: Troubleshooting and Continued Maintenance

Once your solar panels are installed, you want to ensure they function at their maximum capacity. You will not wear out the sun, so take as much advantage of this as possible. If you are having issues, which is rare if the installation was done well, then there are a few areas to look at.

Troubleshooting Tips

The Wiring is Sloppy

Many electrical problems can be traced back to faulty wiring. The wiring connects all of the system's components. As a result, there are numerous places where connections may be loose. You can use specific meters to help pinpoint the issue or retrace your wiring to find any faulty connections.

Overheating of the System

You may notice some heat fade if your panels are overheating due to high temperatures in the upper 90s and above. As a result, your panels may underperform. If overheating is the root cause, you may notice less power during heat waves. This is an issue that should be addressed before installation. Make sure to buy panels that are much more heat resistant. Many of these panels have a thin material sandwiching the microcrystalline layer, making them more efficient at high temperatures than other panels.

The System is Contaminated or Damaged

The most common performance issue is caused by dirt and other debris in your system. Depending on how you look at it, Mother Nature can be a panel's best friend or worst enemy. It is beneficial to hose down your panels at least twice a year. If you notice debris buildup, you can increase the frequency as needed.

In areas with hardened dirt, a soft push broom can be used. You can also hire a cleaning crew. When cleaning a solar panel, do the following:

Never use an abrasive sponge or soap on the glass because they will scratch it.

Avoid Using Harsh Cleaning Products

Exercise extreme caution when getting on the roof because it can become slippery while hosing down your panels.

Consider Buying a Solar Panel Cleaning Kit that Comes with All of the Supplies You Need

If you notice small cracks or damage to the panels, they should be addressed immediately. The panel's functionality will be okay for a while, but the damage will eventually increase and worsen the system. A damaged panel, which is rare, needs to be changed out. If a particular section of a panel can be replaced, that's also an option, depending on the damage.

Regular data monitoring is the easiest way to check your P.V. system's health. This lets you keep tabs on performance factors like power output, array voltage and current, and kWh energy production.

If your array production/power output is lower than average, it could be due to one or more of the following:

- A bad solar panel
- Old batteries (for off-grid systems, batteries may need replacement every five to eight years)
- Shading
- Damaged wiring
- An unusually high temperature lowers panel efficiency
- Dirty modules/debris on panels

What Can Go Wrong with Solar Panels and Wiring?

Under normal conditions, a quality P.V. solar panel placed online today will likely be cranking out electricity at nearly the same rate thirty years from now. When problems do occur, it usually means replacing the panel. Here are some of the issues you might see and what they can indicate:

Cracked glass: Cracks can let water inside the module, possibly leading to corrosion, electrical shorting, and even a shock risk. So, when you see a cracked panel, you need to replace it.

Hot-spotting: Hot-spotting can occur when one cell in a string of cells is consistently shaded, leading to a concentration of power in a small area. Visual clues may include corrosion, cell discoloration, dark spots on cell wiring, melted solder on intercell wiring, or cracked glass. Not to worry, most solar panels today are designed with bypass diodes to help eliminate problems due to shading.

Cracked/broken cell: Physical cell damage often is due to mishandling and is caught during installation, but things like hail and temperature stress can lead to broken or cracked cells after installation.

Discolorations of cells: Cells with a cloudy, whitish appearance may indicate water intrusion, hot-spotting (at its right), or delamination of the cell and glass, although delamination is much less common now than in the past.

If the off-grid system is not producing power at all, it could be due to one or more of the following:

- A tripped breaker. You can visually inspect your system and check for obvious problems, then reset the breaker
- Blown fuse in the combiner box
- Activation of the rapid shutdown
- A failed control board in the inverter

- Someone shut off the P.V. system while working on the home's electrical system and didn't restart the P.V. system

Maintenance Tips

Having a photovoltaic system can be a great way to save energy. But for this to work perfectly, allowing us to transform solar energy into electricity, it is necessary to periodically check the system to keep its productivity levels consistently high and ensure longer life of its components. For the correct functioning of the photovoltaic system, it is, therefore, necessary to take care of its maintenance to prevent a whole series of accidents, such as a fire, which can damage or reduce its performance. It is, therefore, crucial to know your photovoltaic system sufficiently to act at its best and keep it efficient.

First, to ensure proper operation of the panels, they must be kept as clean as possible. Dust, dust, soil, and external elements, such as leaves or birds' nests, can cause the system's malfunction. The deposited dirt can inhibit sunlight's absorption and thus reduce energy accumulation. Seasonal cleaning of solar panels is always recommended. Although rain can help keep the panels clear, it is often not enough, and a more intelligent intervention is needed, which may require using a specific detergent or suitable tools. It is best not to use a too abrasive sponge when cleaning, as this could damage and scratch the structure of the panels. Water, soap, and elbow oil are often sufficient to maintain the system at its best, but there are many kits on the market to ensure you use the right tools. Another important trick is to dry the modules well and avoid leaving halos, which can negatively affect the structure's performance in a lesser way than dirt. To ensure the correct functioning of the system, it is always advisable to monitor the performance obtained. This way, having the situation under control, we can immediately notice anomalies and faults.

The standard everyday cleaning operations are not always simple. If the solar panels are placed in difficult-to-reach areas, such as on a roof, you can use special telescopic tools to assist in cleaning and reaching the most difficult points. However, turning to specialized companies is the best solution, especially for those who are short on time or want to ensure a job well done. Typically, these companies handle system maintenance from start to finish, cleaning and performing a visual inspection to detect any damage, monitoring the system's performance, and ensuring it operates at peak efficiency.

Keep panels out of direct sunlight. If necessary, prune any nearby trees.

Maintain an eye on the inverters to ensure they are always flashing green. If they are not, you are losing money by not substituting for your electricity consumption.

Always document and track the system's daily performance. Every day, record how much energy was produced at a specific time. Make special notes on days when the weather is bad. The manufacturer can provide you with the appropriate monitoring system for your panels.

If you don't have time to clean your panels by hand, you can install automatic cleaners, similar to a sprinkler system. A timer will activate these.

Fortunately, solar panels do not have any moving parts that can rust. As a result, maintenance needs are minimal.

What About Below Ground?

So far, I've been discussing installing solar panels on the roof, which is the ideal location for residential properties. However, solar panels are frequently mounted into the ground when it comes to commercial properties or solar farms. This option is also available for residential homes. In fact, in some cases, it may be the best option. For example, your roof could be completely shaded. Your roof may also be made of a material that does not allow solar panels to be mounted properly. Finally, your roof might not have enough space. There could be various reasons solar panels won't fit on someone's roof. The following are some benefits of installing solar panels on the ground rather than on a rooftop.

The sun is perfectly aligned. Because solar panels work best when facing south, your roof may not always provide this option. Because they can be pointed in almost any direction for optimal sun exposure, ground-mounted panels can eliminate the problem.

If you have a lot of land that gets a lot of sun, you can put it to good use by having your little solar farm. Most people's lawns are larger than their roofs. You can install a relatively large system to generate significant amounts of energy. As before, you will need permits to check your local zoning regulations.

Now that I've covered the benefits, let's look at some of the drawbacks:

Ground-mounted panels are not secured to a pre-existing structure, such as your roof. As a result, before installing your solar panels, you must first construct a secure structure. Lay a concrete foundation to accomplish this. This procedure can increase the time and cost of your investment.

Ground-mounted solar panels are not visually appealing in a residential setting. An efficient ground-mounted system's panels must be several feet above the ground and set at an angle. Nothing is discrete about them, and there is no way to conceal them. Many people will find this an eyesore, and if you decide to sell your home later, the potential buyers may not appreciate having a solar farm in their yard.

The panels will take up most of your yard and block you from doing recreational activities.

What is the Best Time to Clean?

As we have already pointed out, planning a periodic cleaning of the photovoltaic systems is good. The best period to carry out maintenance is the time before the period of increased production. In simple terms, the most suitable time is the beginning of spring. The winter months put a strain on the systems due to the strong temperature fluctuations, cold temperatures, and also because of snowfalls. The weight of the accumulated snow can cause damage to the plant, which should be checked to monitor its proper functioning.

In addition to cleaning the solar panels, which, as we have seen, is an essential element, there are other essential precautions that contribute to maintaining the perfect efficiency of the system. Let's see in detail the different interventions that must be carried out.

Inverter Control

Inverters are the heart of every system. They are how solar energy is converted into electricity. In addition, they are responsible for monitoring the entire system and enabling it to work at peak performance constantly. Usually, they have a 10-year warranty, and the monitoring should be done at the end of the ten years unless a fault occurs. The inverters are overhauled by specialist personnel, who monitor their correct operation and ensure efficiency.

Check Cabling and Electrical Connections

This control should also be entrusted to specialized personnel, who will periodically check that the whole system is working correctly and that there are no faults or problems related to electrical connections.

Checking the Performance of Photovoltaic Modules

The control of the production of solar panels is a handy tool for monitoring the efficiency of the photovoltaic system. A drop in production can indicate problems, such as a failure or the presence of dirt. But the problem may be attributable to damage to one of the cells, which in this case will have to be replaced. A thermal chamber is often used to check the modules, immediately detecting faults and malfunctions.

Checking the Antifreeze Level

Checking the antifreeze level, which helps prevent temperature changes during the winter months from damaging the photovoltaic modules, is also essential to monitor. As we have seen, cold temperatures put stress on the system, which must be able to protect the cells from frost.

Battery Management

Another element that could be considered to reduce maintenance and increase system profitability is the addition of a lithium storage battery. This simple trick allows you to improve the system's efficiency. As the name implies, a storage battery will enable you to store unused solar energy and spend it at times of the day when you are forced to use grid power, such as in the evening and at night. This allows you to reduce your bill costs drastically while using your photovoltaic system best. Furthermore, a storage system requires little maintenance compared to a traditional battery.

Array Cleaning and Inspection

A routine cleaning improves system performance and allows for a close visual inspection of the solar panels, wiring, and other hardware to ensure everything is in working order. The local conditions determine the frequency with which you must clean.

If the weather is dry and there is a lot of dust in the air, cleaning a few times a year may be beneficial. Tree pollen, bird poop, and leaves from trees, which effectively shade solar panels, necessitate cleaning. However, skipping a seasonal cleaning or two for many systems will have little effect on average system performance, especially if rain washes the panels for you. And, if necessary, binoculars can be used to inspect a rooftop array from the ground.

Snow removal is also recommended, but PV solar panels lose their snow cover faster than conventional roofing once the sun comes out. When getting onto a snow-covered roof to sweep snow off your panels, take the following safety precautions: Safety first! For all rooftop work, use fall-arresting equipment.

Using plain water and a non-abrasive sponge or coarse rag, clean the panels from top to bottom. For stubborn spots, use a synthetic scrubby pad, but avoid using metal scrubbers (or any metal tools) or abrasive cleaners, which can scratch the panel glass.

Simply Rinse the Solar Panels with Water

Squeegee the glass to remove any remaining water droplets. (Of course, you don't squeegee after every rainstorm, but rainwater contains very little mineral content, unlike 'hard' municipal water, which deposits minerals.) To reach interior panels, you might want to use a long-handled window cleaning tool (with a sponge and squeegee on one head).

Battery Care for Off-Grid Systems

Some battery banks necessitate routine maintenance. All everyday tasks are watering (refilling the batteries with distilled water), equalization charges, and testing specific gravity and voltage.

While sealed batteries do not require routine maintenance, it is critical to inspect them regularly to check for loose connections or corrosion and to clean the tops as needed.

Watering is usually necessary every four to eight weeks, but schedules vary greatly. When the batteries are new, check the water levels once a month until you know how frequently they need topping off, and then adjust the schedule as needed.

Only use distilled water to refill when the batteries are fully charged.

When the batteries are not fully charged, check the water level and add enough distilled water to cover the exposed plates. After fully charging the batteries, check the water levels and add water to the specified level.

Batteries contain potentially lethal amounts of energy. Take care when cleaning and watering the terminals. Do not use your bare hands to touch the terminals!

Another battery maintenance technique is 'Equalization.' It is a process of overcharging the batteries to reverse the effects of stratification (when acid levels become higher at the bottom of the battery than at the top) and sulfation (a buildup of sulfate crystals on the plates), both of which shorten battery life.

Season Maintenance

Summer Cleaning

Summer is a favorite season for most homeowners because it is extremely productive for solar panels. Nonetheless, homeowners must be aware of the dust, pollen, or animal droppings that may fall on the solar array from time to time. You also can't rely on summer rain showers to clean for you; they won't do as thorough a job as you can. To keep panels clean and efficient, a simple rinse with warm soapy water and a non-abrasive brush should suffice.

Maintenance in the Fall

Solar panels are strong enough to continue producing energy even in the fall. Of course, this is only possible if the panels are not encrusted with leaves, dust, or dirt. Even if there are no large trees near your home, there is no way to keep the leaves from interfering with the power system. The autumn winds, which carry debris and other vegetation in the air and offload them on panels and racking systems, will be your most difficult challenge during the fall season.

Winter Preparation

Many homeowners are concerned that their solar panels will produce little electricity. While receiving full days of sunlight may be difficult during the winter, your solar panels will still absorb as much as they can. There will be days when the sun shines (even if only for a half-day), so make sure there are no obstructions such as snow on panels that can sabotage power production. Removing snow from solar panels may be challenging, especially in areas where snowfall is expected every week during the winter.

In such cases, you must rely on the sun to melt the snow within a day or two of it falling on the panels. However, the panels must be mounted with at least a 15-degree tilt for the snow to melt. Ice buildup should be avoided because it can compromise the integrity of your roof, affecting the structure of your solar power system. I do not recommend that people use salt to melt snow because it could potentially damage the systems, causing the racks and panels to erode. Attempt to remove as much ice as possible manually.

Spring Cleaning

I believe that spring is the best time to perform preventative maintenance on your solar panels. During this time, you can focus on inspecting the installation, wiring, and the health of the inverter and battery bank to address any issues that have arisen.

Chapter 8: Safety Instructions for Handling Solar Power Systems

It is now time to learn how to operate solar power systems safely. The solar kits are the most straightforward installation on your vehicles or home. However, you must take some precautions to avoid casualties.

Ascertain that all of the necessary solar system equipment and tools are available. Fuse and fuse holders, solar panels, inverters, mounts, wires, charge controllers, and batteries are among them.

Before we learn about solar system safety precautions, here is a list of the contents of a solar kit.

Contents of the Solar Kit

- Charge controller for solar panels
- The solar controller is connected to the battery circuit
- Solar panels (at least 100 watts or 150 watts)
- Foot mounting hardware includes an 11 mm bolt, an 11 mm hex nut, a washer, and a lock
- Solar panel black to controller wire
- Solar panel red to controller wire
- Solar Installation Tools and Equipment
- Philips screwdriver and 11-millimeter wrench
- Self-leveling sealant
- A reciprocating saw is used to make a flush-mounting controller
- Drill and drill bit 3/8 inch

Choose How You Want to Install Your Solar System

Make enough room to install all of the solar system's components. The kit includes thirty feet of wire. This consists of a wire run of fifteen feet from the solar charge controller to the battery. Another 15 feet connects the PV panels to the charge controller. The solar charge controller is only visible from the outside.

However, lay down some wood, fiberglass, rubber, or tin if you want to install the panel on a van, RV, or car. If you're connecting the panel to an off-grid station, ensure it's facing the sun during peak sunlight hours. This will improve its overall efficiency throughout the day. However, for optimal performance, their positions must be adjusted frequently.

Route or Map Out the Path that the Wire will Take

To ensure proper wiring, it is necessary to map out the direction of the wires from the start. This also allows you to drill the required holes and route the wires. If the wires' other ends are larger than 3/8 inch, the small ring terminals on the wires must be fed from the other ends. Seal any holes in the roof with self-leveling sealant. There should be no wires connected to the solar panel or battery.

Drill and Cut Holes for the Charge Controller

Cut and drill any holes required for the circuit system to function. You'll see symbols like + - on the solar charge controller. The battery also has + - marks. These are the connections that are both positive and negative. Connect the battery's positive terminal to the solar panel's positive terminal before connecting the negative terminals. This could be accomplished with a Philips screwdriver. Check that all of the solar charge controller's connections are secure. Then, on the surface, tighten the solar charge controller.

Install the Solar Panel Mounting Feet

Screw the mounting feet to the solar panel using the hardware and an 11-millimeter wrench. This installation may necessitate the use of two wrenches. Both the lock washer and the bolt must be threaded. Feed it through the PV panels and the mounting foot holes. Before tightening the screws, connect the hex nut and flat washer.

Install the solar panel on any surface you want using the appropriate tools. Using the self-leveling sealant, keep the mounting feet firmly attached to the surface. Also, don't forget to seal and cover the tops of the screws at the end of your installations.

Connect the positive wire to the positive axis of the battery using a fuse. Similarly, use a fuse to connect the negative wire to the negative axis of the battery. Check that the wire connections are firm and tight.

If you're using many batteries, try to connect them in the way I described above. Following these connections, your solar system is ready to generate electricity.

You can also consult your user manual to learn more about configuring the charge controller to regulate the battery and other features and functionalities.

Procedures for Shutting Down and Restarting

Before working on any wiring, always turn off the PV system and make sure the power is turned off. Even small residential PV systems generate more than enough electricity to kill! Accidents can be avoided by turning off the power before working on or maintaining the system. To shut down the entire PV system, follow the proper procedure. Before touching any wires while working on or near wiring, use a multimeter to confirm that the power is turned off.

Never connect or disconnect wires while they are under load. The term "load" refers to anything that draws power from an electrical circuit, causing current to flow. Interrupting the circuit while the current is flowing is dangerous.

Disconnect switches and breakers are the primary shutdown devices for PV systems. The A.C disconnect on most systems can be locked out in the 'Switched Off' position by securing the switch arm with a padlock.

While working on the household system, locking out the A.C. disconnect switch prevents another person from turning on the power to the house. If a switch has a lockout feature, use it. Different systems have slightly different shutdown procedures, and it's critical to understand which parts of the system are disabled 'at zero voltage' and which are not.

Turning off the A.C. disconnect, for example, turns off the power to the microinverters, effectively shutting down everything except the solar panels and their wire leads on a microinverter system.

With a string inverter or off-grid system, activating the rapid shutdown disconnect turns off the power at the disconnecting combiner box within ten feet of the array. The array and all the wiring between the panels and the combiner box remain life. The only way to make your solar panel stop producing electricity is to cover it entirely so that no light gets through. But that is rarely necessary for routine system maintenance.

If the system has a generator, turn off the generator disconnect to shut down A.C power input and disable an auto-start function.

Activate the shutdown button or switch on the P.V. system's rapid shutdown control box. If the off-grid system does not have a rapid shut down, turn off all D.C disconnects from the P.V. array.

Move the switch on the system A.C disconnect to the 'OFF' position, and lock it out. This ensures that the inverter is not under load.

Switch the D.C disconnect for the inverter to the 'OFF' position. This ensures the inverter cannot provide A.C output.

Turn off the D.C main disconnect, which will shut down the P.V. charge controller.

How to power on an off-grid system

Turn on the D.C main disconnect, which will turn on the charge controller or the battery bank breakers.

Switch the D.C disconnect for the inverter to the 'ON' position.

Move the switch on the system A.C disconnect to the 'ON' position.

If the system has a generator, turn 'ON' the generator disconnect to start A.C power input and enable any auto-start function.

Other Safety Rules for Handling Solar Installations

1. Do not work in bad weather. It is not advisable to handle solar installations in bad weather conditions such as during rains, fogs, and mists. This could cause electric shock, or if you must work, ensure that you wear the appropriate personal protective equipment like non-slip shoes, helmets, and gloves. Again, the windy climate can destabilize the panels by blowing them around or blowing them off completely. This could cause the panels to fall and get damaged.
2. Avoid sitting or standing on solar panels. Do not drop any heavy objects on the panels too. This pressure can break the glassy coverings and cause injuries. Also, the pressure could damage the panels and cause electric shock.
3. Ensure the home's sheathing is not wet. This can cause leakage in your roof. New buildings usually experience this problem, even old houses. It could happen if the shingles are removed during installation.
4. Ensure that the area beneath your solar panels is clean.
5. Avoid installing your solar panels in a corrosive environment. This type of location is marked C5 by International Standard Organization (ISO).
6. If you are working on rooftops, ensure that you have lifelines, safety nets, and harnesses.
7. Apply insulated tools whenever you are working on a solar system.
8. Avoid using magnified or artificial lights on the solar system.
9. Do not mount your PV panels close to flammable gas outlets to avoid explosion and fire.
10. Do not put on metallic jewelry while working on solar installations.

11. Use opaque materials to cover the panels while working on the circuit system. This will prevent the production of electricity.
12. If you are in a location within 0.3 miles from a sea or ocean, do not install your PV panels. Salty mists and vapors can affect your panels and cause electric shock or damage.
13. Mount your photovoltaic panels on a strong roof that can hold the devices securely.
14. Before installing a PV panel, ensure that the entire device is properly and safely earthed to prevent electrocution.
15. Adhere to all electricity installation guidelines in your community. Your local power authority can advise you further.
16. Check all the ladders and scaffolds before using them.
17. Do not work in windy or snowy terrains. This is to avoid falling or slipping from heights.
18. Examine all your power tools to ascertain that they are functioning correctly.
19. Working on rooftops demands extra caution.
20. Do not work with wet tools, slippery conditions, or after rainfall.
21. Apply duct seal or waterproof fittings to stop moisture from slipping into the conduit system. This will damage the panels.
22. If the circuit system passes through walls, ensure to attach the metal conduit to cover wires exposed to rainfall, sunlight, and wind. This will prevent short circuits or shock in the system.
23. Avoid locations with falling objects.
24. Scaffolds are recommended for you to use if you must climb to a height 6 feet or more above the ground surface. Do not use ladders for such heights.
25. Engage a partner that should hold the ladder for you while you are climbing to install the panel.

26. Connect an earthing or grounding wire from the installed panels to the ground. This will prevent electric shock.

Chapter 9: Choosing the Right System for your Car

What is a Solar Car?

As its name implies, a solar car is a kind of automobile powered by the sun. Solar cars can be likened to hybrids. They will still run on electricity. However, they differ because hybrid cars do not eliminate the use of gas. Second, they do not possess one of the critical components solar vehicles have: solar panels.

Solar cars have wider bodies because they require many solar panels to function. These panels are made up of photovoltaic cells arranged in a module. A single vehicle can have hundreds or thousands of arrays or modules.

One of the most significant advantages of solar cars is that they eliminate the need for gasoline. The constant fluctuation of gas prices, as well as large suppliers who tend to dictate the cost in the global market, is untrustworthy.

Owners are not required to charge their vehicles regularly, which consumes a significant amount of their time, as with hybrids or electric vehicles. Second, the power source is renewable. Because the sun is expected to burn for billions of years, the energy required is constantly replenished.

But are solar cars being mass-produced today? Unfortunately, there aren't any yet. The majority of those you see in glossies, news articles, and on the Internet are prototypes, which are unfinished and still in the development or research stages. Though the benefits are enormous, the challenges are equally so.

One of the major issues is the cost of production. Solar panels are not cheap, even today. A large sum of money is required to design solar panels that allow the car to run like other cars. When the cost of production is high, so is the selling price. Only the wealthiest can benefit from technology.

Creating solar-powered cars will also necessitate a significant change in production assembly, which will incur additional costs. Of course, each automobile component must be designed and mass-produced.

The primary design of the solar car comes next. They have expanded sides to accommodate the solar panels, as previously stated. It becomes a major issue once the vehicle enters congested lanes and intersections. Roads are not designed to accommodate large vehicles. Furthermore, solar cars can only carry one person at a time because extra weight requires more power to maintain the car's speed.

Despite these issues, there is still a lot of interest in solar cars. Instead, it remains one of the most discussed engineering solutions by the government and experts.

Solar car races are always anticipated in certain parts of the world. In South Africa, the Solar Challenge attracts some of the toughest car competitors and legions of fans and spectators eager to see futuristic car designs and the true capabilities of solar-powered cars. Competing teams design and manufacture their vehicles during the two-week race, which is held twice a year.

Solar power was once considered a theory, a principle, or even a figment of someone's wild imagination. However, recent developments indicate that it may have a future after all.

The installation of your solar charging system is divided into three stages. The first step is to determine the system size you need and whether you will be charging only your vehicle or your entire home.

The second stage is installation, which can appear to be the most difficult but is very simple if you follow the step-by-step instructions. Finally, you must set up, use, and monitor your electricity generation and consumption; this will tell you if your initial calculations were correct!

One of the greatest hurdles to overcome when attempting to power an electric car from a solar charger is how it can recharge the vehicle after a long trip.

Home-Based System

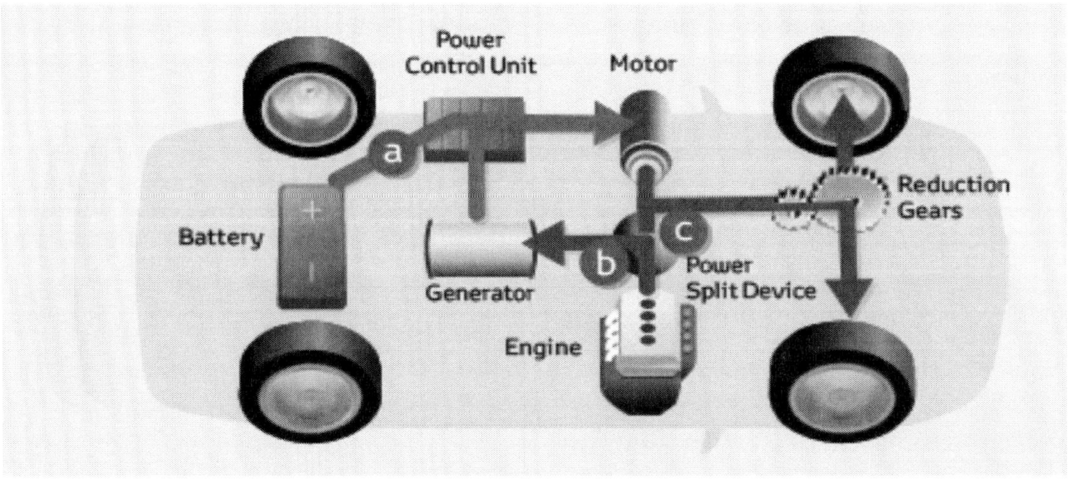

The most obvious route is to equip your home with solar panels and use the electricity generated to charge your electric car batteries. This is generally considered the best option for anyone with an electric car. The amount of electricity it takes to recharge a car every night will significantly increase your electricity bill's overall cost. This can even push the rate you pay per unit up.

You should already know how much the car will cost to charge; this is an important part of your calculations before buying a vehicle. If you have not looked into this and already purchased an electric car, you will likely notice the additional electricity cost on your monthly bill.

This is valuable information to help you choose the right one for your needs and power costs if you want to purchase an electric car.

Understanding the Electricity Required to Power Your Car

Every type of electric car will have its electricity rating. You will see it in the dealer or can locate the statistics online. The figure you need to look for is its kilowatt-hours (kWh) rating. This figure shows how much electricity is required to allow the vehicle to drive one hundred miles. An average vehicle will require approximately 30kWh; however, this will vary depending upon the performance of the vehicle, its size, and its shape.

There are two important calculations you can look at from this; both of them will require you to know your average annual mileage:

Cost Comparison to Gas

You should be able to work out your average yearly mileage. If you do not know it, simply calculate the miles you cover in an average week and multiply it by fifty-two.

You will also need to know the cost of your electricity per unit, the price of a gallon of fuel, and the miles per gallon your vehicle will do.

You will then be able to calculate your costs:

- **Electricity:** Annual mileage of 12,000 / 100 * the kWh rating of your vehicle; for example, the average of 30 will do. The resulting figure of 3,600 can then be multiplied by the cost per unit of electricity. For example, if you pay .12 cents per unit, it will be $432 to run your car for the year.

- **Gas:** This time, your annual mileage will need to be divided by the average number of miles per gallon your car does. This will give you the number of gallons of fuel you need. Simply multiply by the cost per gallon (approximately $2.40), and you will have your comparison cost for the year. 12,000 / 35 * 2.40 equals $805; a substantial difference.

Of course, other factors are involved, such as the cost of charging your vehicle away from home. But the figures will give an idea of the cost savings you can generate.

Electricity Usage

The second calculation will simply illustrate how much power you need. This is merely the first part of the cost comparison equation. Your annual mileage is divided by 100 and then multiplied by the kWh of your vehicle. In the above example, this equates to 3600kW of electricity per year.

You can further divide this by 52 to get your approximate weekly requirements; 69.23 kWh.

Interestingly, the average American home will use approximately 8,000kWh per year; charging your electric car at home could add half your current bill to the yearly charge.

It is essential to understand how much electricity your vehicle will likely use. You can fit panels accordingly if you plan to generate enough power just to charge your electric car. If this is in addition to powering your home, this figure must be considered when calculating the number of solar panels required.

Dedicated Car System

The second option is to install solar panels that will only be used to power your car. If you prefer, you can do this without connecting to the grid. However, this may imply that a large portion of the electricity generated will be wasted. This is not a viable option unless you install the system on a tight budget and intend to expand it in the future. As the figures above show, the cost of a small system can be recouped in a few years, especially if you follow this guide and install most of the components yourself.

Some research and testing have been done on systems that can be installed in your vehicle to recharge or trickle charge while driving. The goal is to enable you to travel for longer periods without having to pay and recharge along the way.

This system will likely appeal only to people who frequently travel long distances. This option discussed later in the book is unlikely to be justified by staying close to home and taking an annual vacation.

Once you start tracking your daily electric car usage, you may be surprised at how little you need and how few miles you travel!

The system decision will allow you to start planning the installation, but you should also consider the power of the sun in your specific area. The more sunlight you have, the better your power generation; if you live in a cloudy area, you may not have enough electricity to meet your needs during winter. It is best to calculate this before starting your installation, as it may affect the number of panels you use.

The average solar panel will generate 250 watts of electricity in ideal conditions. Consider how much you need daily to determine how many will be required to power your electric car. Based on the preceding example, this should be around 10kWh per day.

Then, figure out how much sunlight you get on an average day; this will vary depending on where you live. Divide your 10kWh by five to get two if you get five hours of sunlight per day. This is the kilowatts you must generate daily to meet your vehicle's needs.

Before you finish your calculation, keep in mind that solar energy is converted into direct current (DC), which must then be converted into alternating current (AC) for use at home. This results in a 20% reduction in your power. This must be considered in your calculations. 2kw divided by.8 equals 2.5.

You will need ten solar panels to generate 2.5kw of electricity using 250-watt panels; this will be enough to power your vehicle. If you want to contribute to or cover the cost of electricity in your home, you must factor in your home usage.

Solar Power Battery Charger

Many people are searching for ways to use energy proficient, leading the wave toward eco-friendly and environmentally friendly alternative energy sources.

Even though charges are a discouraging factor for most, Solar Power Battery is a step in a good direction.

Solar Power Charger is a good idea! Naturally, the system would be better if we had better batteries. Still, solar battery chargers can be a good choice for operating devices at home and as part of your workplace.

As the term suggests, solar is the energy acquired from the sun. Solar Battery works with lots of various other solar gizmos.

Portable batteries imply you do not need to worry about whether you can power the unit inside a foreign nation or during a vacation in the United States. Portable solar battery chargers are already a significant advantage to many adventurous individuals.

They will no longer have to pack in many extra batteries when planning to go on trips. Portable solar chargers are readily available and constructed into many small products. The truth is that solar-driven calculators have been about for many years.

Solar battery chargers are the most effective, allowing you to charge your batteries without paying for the additional power obtained. Solar battery casings are manufactured from resilient, lightweight materials with a lower heat transmittance. These enclosures shield the batteries from overheating, weather conditions, and thieves.

Solar power battery chargers are available for every size and also sorts of batteries. Solar power battery backups are widely used in homes, allowing people to remain updated on the outside world during disasters and even routine blackouts.

Solar power battery banks, a series of batteries that have been wired with each other inside the solar panel system, are necessary if you need an energy system that works proficiently and is also cost-efficient.

Setting up a solar panel can be pretty simple because it's readily available. Installing an alternate energy alternative at home is a very good humanitarian effort. One of many alternative power options, solar energy, and wind energy systems are the most favored, being less complicated.

Solar panels are rated in watts. A regular 15-watt panel will certainly generate around 1 amp of power. The solar power battery technology for chargers is consistently being enhanced, mainly because we realize there's a chance for better energy or a source of energy.

Charging periods are usually only estimations and depend on numerous variables such as device, weather, spot, and exposure angle. Charge the unit at any place, anytime.

Portable solar chargers allow us to maintain small electric devices, for instance, cell phones, iPods, and digital cameras. Hardly any other electric source is necessary if you have enough sun to supply energy.

If you cannot afford many solar panels to power your home, it is achievable to lower your energy expenses simply by using a Solar Battery to recharge the batteries.

Solar Powered Accessories

Solar power was highly advertised as an excellent energy alternative, but it hasn't hit the sweet spot in popularity because not the technology was too expensive. Things are a bit different nowadays because plenty of solar power accessories are sold today. Calculators and watches were typical examples of solar accessories in the past, but big companies are moving on to release more serious products like keyboards and even netbooks. These accessories all share the same benefits of solar in general, so it is best to take note.

Energy is produced and stored by relying on solar panels to collect energy from the sun. That energy is converted into usable energy through a generator. Since nothing needs to be burned, no harmful pollutants are produced. As a result, making solar accessories environmentally friendly because the sun has virtually infinite amounts of energy, you can recharge your solar power accessories as often as you like without relying on other sources of electricity so long as you do not mind recharging the batteries now and then.

There are hardly any moving parts regarding solar generators or internal components of solar accessories. No sound is produced when the panel collects energy from the sun and transfers the energy to a battery for storage. Any accessories that rely on solar power are safer because they often strive for eco-friendliness. Hence, you will not be worried about harmful side effects or undergo complicated procedures to stay safe while operating these accessories.

Saying that this power is inexpensive can raise a lot of eyebrows. But the reality is that there are a good number of cheap components that can turn any accessory into a solar-powered accessory. You need to do some proper online research so you can find DIY guides or other tutorials on how to build a solar power accessory from scratch.

Solar power accessories may be a bit more expensive if you do not prefer making these yourself. However, you will save some money by not relying on non-renewable sources.

Types of Solar Power Modules

Monocrystalline Solar Cells

These solar module panels are made up of thin slices of silicon arranged in a grid to form a panel. However, this is the most helpful panel type because it can collect more energy. Furthermore, it is the most expensive type. It is the best panel for limited areas that are smaller than average. It has a longer shelf life.

Polycrystalline Solar Cells

While less expensive than monocrystalline solar cells, they are also less efficient. It can be cost-effective. As a result, it is recommended for wide and larger areas. Silicon takes the form of interlocking crystals, which are less expensive to produce. It has a longer life span than an amorphous screen.

Amorphous Solar Cells

This solar panel performs best in cold, cloudy, and dark conditions. They are the most recent in a long line of solar panels and are made through a complicated process. Because they are flexible, they can be bent to follow curves and outlines on the roof. They are commonly used in calculators. It may be a viable alternative to crystalline cells.

The performance capacity of a solar module panel is determined by its construction. Getting the best material means getting the best service that people can afford. Knowing that we have solar module panels today, we can easily choose which model fits our budget and requirements. If you're looking for a panel for your home, a model for home use will be very different from those for camping and boating. The most expensive type will perform better if you want a less costly solar module panel.

When selecting a module, the screen's durability should be considered. Make sure to inquire about the life expectancy of each panel that they provide. A less expensive model may last for a decade, while a more expensive model may have a 20-25-year warranty. It is usually preferable to determine the framing materials used to determine the structure's longevity. The more we can use a panel, the more money we save. So, when selecting a solar module panel, understand it before you trust it. Compare prices and choose the best deal.

Chapter 10: What Happens if you Move?

Just like solar panels can be installed in one location, they can be removed and transferred to another area. Therefore, you can take your solar panels if you decide to move. Of course, this can come with its own set of challenges. Moving solar panels and equipment is not an easy process, so make sure you do the proper research before you start dismantling.

Before you decide to move your solar panels, there are a few things you need to consider to make sure it will be worth it. This can be a grueling process, so it's essential to make sure you are taking everything into account before you make a move. Make sure you are still taking advantage of all the benefits.

Are You Thinking About Selling Your Home?

It is natural to want to take your solar panels with you if you are selling your current home and moving to a new one. After all, you put a lot of money into them. However, keep in mind that the value of your home can increase significantly, and selling for a higher price can offset the cost of your solar panels. Before you put your house on the market, calculate the potential return and decide whether it's even worth it to remove your panels. It might be easier to leave them in place and install new ones when you move.

If you sell the property with the solar panels still attached, you will no longer be able to keep them. Consider whether you will sell your home with the solar panels attached or not.

Logistics and Location

The new location to which you are relocating significantly impacts whether you should relocate your solar panels. If you are moving nearby, ask the company that delivered and/or installed your equipment if they will move it for you. This is preferable to transporting everything yourself or hiring a general moving company.

If having the original installers or manufacturers move the equipment is not an option, it may be in your best interest to leave it where it is and simply try to sell it for a higher price. Solar panel removal and reinstallation is a time-consuming process. Many businesses may not even remove them due to warranty concerns. Purchasing new panels for your new home may be a more practical solution.

New Location Rules and Regulations

Contact the electric company in your new location to learn about their solar panel rules and regulations, particularly regarding reinstallations. This is also where you'll learn about zoning and permit requirements. Make sure you have permission to move your solar panels to your new home.

Availability of the Sun

The availability of sun exposure in the area was a significant factor in deciding to go solar. Determine whether the availability will be equal, or at least close, before moving to your new location. Before relocating your solar panels, consider the various weather conditions and locations.

Potential Harm

Even though solar equipment is quite durable, the possibility of damage exists. Always keep this in mind when moving your equipment. Moving solar panels requires excellent skill and experience, so proceed with caution. If the solar panels are more than ten years old, it is probably not worth the effort to relocate them.

Be prepared for roof damage as well. The area under the panels will retain its color, whereas the area outside of the panel's edges will be discolored due to natural wear from direct sunlight. Furthermore, small holes in the roofing material will be left as panels are removed. If you intend to sell your home and take your panels with you, these issues must be addressed with the buyer. If they decide to buy the house after the panels are removed, they may expect you to repair the roof. This will be another expense that may or may not be worthwhile.

Before deciding to relocate your solar equipment, consider all of these issues. Again, selling everything along with the house may be more practical in terms of time and money.

Safe Moving Procedures

If you are determined to relocate your solar panels and do not want to leave them behind, the complete removal and reinstallation process, including all paperwork, can take three to four months. The basic steps for dismantling an existing solar power system are as follows. Put on your safety goggles and gloves before you begin.

- Take some large opaque cloths and cover all of the solar panels completely. This will block the sunlight and cause the panels to stop producing electricity.

- Set up your voltage meter to measure direct current. Connect the metal portion of the meter's red positive probe to the positive terminal of the solar panel. Connect the metal portion of the black negative probe to the solar panel's negative terminal.
- The meter should show zero volts. Do not dismantle the system until it has done so; otherwise, you risk electric shock.
- Unplug the wires that connect the solar panels to the solar panel system. While holding the wires in place, loosen the bolts or screws.
- Some systems will include an additional solar power disconnect for added security if one of the panels becomes exposed to sunlight.
- Wrap electrical tape or a rubber terminal cover around the ends of each wire. This avoids physical contact if the wires become life. Cover the solar panel wire connections as well.
- You can now carefully remove the equipment and detach the solar panels from this location, including the platforms and conduit.

As you can see, it is not as simple as simply disassembling everything. A system must be dismantled with the same care that it was installed with. This is for your own and the equipment's safety.

Appropriate Transportation

After you have dismantled your solar equipment, it is time to transport it to your new location. To avoid damage to your solar materials, especially the panels, adequate care must be taken during transportation. The following is a list of the materials you will need to package your solar panels safely.

Use the original palette that came with the solar panels when they were first delivered to you. This will provide enough stability and load capacity for the panels.

The underlayment of corrugated cardboard is placed on top of the palette.

Four stacking devices per panel.

Each panel has six foam pads.

Edge protectors come in a pack of eight.

Four pieces of tension belts and straps.

Cover foil: One piece measuring approximately 2,000,1,300x0.04mm.

Safety labeling adhesive tape with pictograms.

To prevent stacking, use a cardboard protection pyramid.

After gathering all of your equipment, proceed with the following packaging steps:

Before using your palette, inspect it for apparent damage.

Place your palette on a stable and flat surface. Consider the space required for handling and final transport.

On the palette, place the corrugated cardboard underlay. Check that it is flush.

Place the solar panel on the cardboard underlay with the front side facing the palette and the back side facing the sun. Make sure it is centered on the palette and not protruding from the edges.

Place two foam pads on each long side and one on each short side of the six foam pads.

Place one stacking device on each of the panel's four corners.

Continue stacking the remaining panels in the same way. On a single palette, you can stack up to 30 panels.

Place the top palette with the front side facing up.

Place two edge protectors in each package corner.

Apply two straps to the long and short sides, close to the palette outer blocks, as tightly as possible without putting too much stress on the panels.

Cover and wrap the package using the material in the list provided above.

Label the packaging with the following labels:

- Fragile
- Keep dry

- Do not stack
- Do not tilt

You can also just use the tape with the pictograms on it.

Wrap the entire panel packaging with the foil. It is recommended to wrap around 35 times on all sides for adequate thickness.

Bond the cover foil to the packaging with adhesive tape. Again, this is the tape with the pictograms of the transport instructions.

Bond the cardboard protection pyramid to the top of the package.

From here, the package of solar panels is ready to be transported. Like before, if you have reservations about doing this safely, I advise hiring the proper movers who are experienced in transporting solar equipment. If you cannot find someone, it may behoove you to leave the equipment behind. Once you are at your new location, it will be time to reinstall the panels again after getting all the necessary permits.

Warranties

With the installation, movement, and maintenance issues that will arise, it is important to have a general idea of how the warranties on solar panels work. You want to avoid getting blindsided as much as possible. The following are some general guidelines for coverage provided on solar panels. Of course, you want to do your research when you buy solar panels. Remember that if you buy used panels or move with them, the warranties could become void. Make sure you find out about all of these coverage details.

Manufacturer's Warranty

There are two specific manufacturer warranties: a performance warranty and a product warranty. The performance warranty guarantees that the panels will not degrade below a specified level. This ensures that the equipment will continue to produce the needed power during the warranty period, which usually ranges between 25 to 30 years. The panels should still work at about 79-87% of the original performance.

The manufacturer does not guarantee a certain amount of solar production for your system. Many variables are at play here, so the performance warranty cannot ensure this aspect. However, you will be assured that each panel can produce a specific amount of instantaneous power on its own.

For example, if your solar panel is in an area with adequate sunlight and was correctly installed but still does not produce the desired output, there might be something functionally wrong. The solar panels could be faulty, which would be covered under the performance warranty.

The product warranty is in place to protect in the case of defective materials or issues with workmanship during the manufacturing process. Per their discretion, the manufacturer can repair the damage or replace the whole product.

The product warranty does not cover the cost of labor to diagnose problems with a product. The labor cost to replace the equipment or shipment of new products will also not be covered. Product warranties generally last between 15-25 years.

As far as the other equipment, the breakdown goes as follows:

- Inverters come with a ten to a 25-year product warranty.
- Batteries come with a warranty of about five to ten years.
- Racking comes with a ten to a 20-year warranty on workmanship and defects in the material.

Solar Installer Guarantee

Some solar installation companies will offer additional protection for the services they provide. Not only will these cover workmanship, but they can also guarantee the total solar production of your system. This goes well beyond a performance warranty. A solar installer guarantee will make sure your product is performing and not just capable of achieving.

A Solar Panel Warranty Becoming Voided

A solar power warranty can become void, so make sure you understand the rules to not allow this to happen. If you lose your warranty too early, you are on the hook for a significant expense without entirely using your solar panels. The following are a few reasons why your warranties can become void:

- Not having them professionally installed. Having work done by a contractor who is not industry certified can nullify a performance warranty. The manufacturer may be unable to tell if it's faulty equipment or poor installation. If someone does install your panels for you, make sure to ask about a solar installation guarantee.
- Failing to maintain your solar panels adequately can also lead to warranty problems. For example, failing to keep branches trimmed or not getting rid of debris can affect your performance warranty.
- Ask your manufacturer and any contractor you hire to give you a list of things that can void the warranty. Remember that your homeowner's insurance will also cover some repairs, so update your insurance agent/company as soon as you buy solar equipment.
- One last recommendation I will make is to ensure you stay at your current location for a long time before installing solar panels. This way, you will get full use of them. Of course, if you are a good investor, perhaps you can use them to increase your property's sale and rental values.

Conclusion

Thank you for reading this book. To build your power grid in the future, you will need to learn how electricity works to build and repair your devices.

Solar power is not only good for the environment, but it is also one of the best energy alternatives in this challenging economic climate. Traditional energy creation requires resources, manpower, and money that can be used for other purposes. Many people are put off by the high installation costs of solar panels. However, when you compare the benefits and prices, you will see that solar panels are more cost-effective in the long run.

If the initial costs are too high for your budget, consider getting a solar panel loan or designing your solar PV module. Search the internet for a used solar panel or try to design your PV module. There are numerous methods for obtaining the solar module.

Modern technology has made solar systems more efficient than earlier technology with limitations. Call a solar panel mount expert and have the panel adequately installed on the roof for the best solar panel exploration.

Because of advances in solar technology, it is now possible to harness the sun's power even when it is cloudy outside. Choose solar PV modules with high-efficiency solar cells to maximize the power of the sun's rays.

Aside from the guide and tips you've read above, it's best if you work with confidence. At first glance, seeing all the technical solar equipment can be intimidating, but you can attack this issue confidently.

Solar energy is "environmentally friendly" because it uses renewable energy sources and avoids generating harmful waste during active use. The engineering construction of photovoltaic technology is functional for converting solar radiation into electrical energy. The methods for converting solar radiation vary according to the design of the power plant.

After studying this material, it is necessary to follow some binding principles for the best solar panel for your home. You must determine the magnitude of the largest energy consumed by household devices that work simultaneously, considering the addition to the starting power.

The presence of this book does not absolve specialists of the need to use normative and technical documentation in the detailed study of certain issues related to designing electrical installations and construction sites. The variety of conditions that must be considered when designing solar power plants prevents us from making specific recommendations on some issues. They must be resolved by examining the requirements for Solar Electric Supply design and construction. As a result, the recommendations in the book should not be regarded as the only ones that could be made.

You should also be patient when installing your off-grid solar system because Rome was not built in a day. It may take a few days to configure your off-grid solar system fully. Don't push yourself too hard, or you'll quickly become frustrated.

You can create an off-grid solar power system to keep you and your loved ones warm and comfortable during your outdoor stay. Solar energy is a fantastic idea. The concept of harnessing solar energy and utilizing it to power electrical power equipment is brilliant. The sun directly or indirectly supports all life forms and provides all of the energy we require to exist.

As a do-it-yourself enthusiast, you can proceed to set up your off-grid solar system once you have everything you need. You do not need technical assistance to set up a functional off-grid solar system because solar system assembly has progressed to the point where they are plug-and-play.

So, I'll say goodbye now and wish you great success and good luck.

Manufactured by Amazon.ca
Acheson, AB

10460749R00087